THE
ADVENTURE
ALTERNATIVE

THE
ADVENTURE
ALTERNATIVE

COLIN MORTLOCK

CICERONE PRESS POLICE SQUARE MILNTHORPE CUMBRIA
ENGLAND

ISBN - 1 85284 012 9
Reprinted 2004

Adventure Ways

The following journeys, providing you take any of them to the outer limits of your capabilities in a self reliant manner, can take you along the road to truth and beauty, freedom and happiness.

UP A MOUNTAIN OR DOWN A RIVER

ACROSS AN OCEAN OR ALONG A COASTLINE

ACROSS THE WILDERNESS OR ALONG THE OUTDOOR WAY

THROUGH THE AIR OR UNDER THE SURFACE OF THE EARTH

Your success is determined by your efforts and not by results, and you may come to realise that the most important journey is the journey inwards.

Contents

Foreword

Colin Mortlock is more than an outdoor educationalist. He is a leading and pioneering adventurer in his own right both in the field of mountaineering and also long distance sea canoeing. In addition he is a thinker and has brought to outdoor education a stimulating, at times controversial, yet very expansive approach to this field.

Colin is an educationalist in the very widest sense. He does not want to place adventure in the outdoors into a tidy little compartment but rather, in his regard for life as a whole as a constant educative process, sees what significance the search for adventure can have on not only broadening mind and body but also in helping us have better, happier and certainly more fulfilled lives.

He grasps and understands the fact that adventure in its very essence has a real element of risk. It is the mastery of this risk that provides one important ingredient in the satisfaction and value of the adventure. Colin Mortlock has helped and encouraged many hundreds of youngsters to discover in themselves abilities and potential that they never realised they could have. Paradoxically, in allowing youngsters to develop their full potential and through this expose themselves to a level of risk which they were able to understand and harness, he was probably also giving them a safer introduction to the outdoors than is given in a much more supervised and heavily controlled environment by many outdoor educationalists who, through the very fact of their cocooning, all too often fail to arm the student against the reality of danger that so many of the adventure-orientated activities must inevitably have. Nearly everyone has a seed of adventure within them waiting to germinate. Colin Mortlock recognises that the level of adventure to which each person might want to aspire is very different in every individual. Reaching towards this feeling of adventure, be it the unknown of a Lakeland hill or some sheltered coastal water, the heights of Everest or the empty, storm-swept coast of Alaska, there is a vast satisfaction and fulfilment to be found in the outdoors. This book delves not only into the philosophy of adventure but a philosophy for life itself.

Chris Bonington
Hesket Newmarket

Preface

Writing this book has been rather like preparing for my first expedition. I now know that, perhaps like any skill, the skill of writing can only be acquired by a considerable amount of hard work over a long period of time. I have been particularly conscious also, of the difficulty of even beginning to coherently define some of the deeper values implicit in the wilderness journey. There have been occasions when I have felt that it was unrealistic to attempt such a book, especially at a time when I was substantially involved practically in the outdoors. So little appears to have been written in this area, however, that it has seemed necessary to make a start.

The book is in two main sections. The first six chapters are concerned with establishing a broad framework of levels of adventure as well as emphasizing the importance both of the quality of the experience and of the possibilities of adventure being instinctive. Subsequent chapters develop a personal philosophy of the potential values of these experiences. Whilst the ideas are essentially from personal experience I have made extensive use of quotations from more authoritative sources. The people whose writings I have used, have inspired me by their own experiences. I hope they also add support to the idea that the key human virtues are crucial to any satisfying lifestyle, and that the outdoor journey in particular has considerable potential in this respect.

Colin Mortlock

Acknowledgements

I am indebted to various friends and colleagues who have rendered invaluable help in commenting on the original text. In particular I would like to thank my wife Annette, Jack Parker and Dr. John Carnie from the Charlotte Mason College, John Wyatt, Chris. Lloynes and Steve Stephenson. I would also like to thank the Library staff of the College for help in the location of quotation material.

Every effort has been made to contact all sources quoted in the text and no slight is intended where this has not proved possible. For permission to use selected extracts, grateful acknowledgement and thanks are extended to the following authors and publishers:

George Allen & Unwin, *My Life & Thought* by A. Schweitzer; The Association of Experiential Education, USA; The Bodley Head, *'North West Passage'* by Willy de Roos; Marion Boyars Publishers Ltd., *The Betrayal of Youth'* by D. Hemming; Cambridge University Press, *Adventures of Ideas* by Prof. A. N. Whitehead; The Literary Estate of F. Spencer Chapman & Chatto & Windus Ltd., for selections from *Memoirs of a Mountaineer;* Collins Publishers, *The Inner Hebrides* by Prunella Stack; J. M. Dent & Sons Ltd., *Lord Jim* by J. Conrad; Doubleday, USA, *The Identity of Man* by Prof. J. Bronowski; HRH The Duke of Edinburgh; Faber & Faber Publishers, *Markings* by Dag Hammarksjold trans. by W. H. Auden and Lief Sjoberg; John Farquharson Ltd., *Oars across the Pacific* by J. Fairfax, and *The Naked Island* by R. Braddon; Victor Gollancz Ltd., *The Great Days* by W. Bonatti; Granada Publishing Limited, *The Long Way* by B. Moittoissier; Harper & Row Publishers Inc., *Profiles in Courage* Memorial Ed. by J. F. Kennedy, and *Foundations for a Theory of Instruction* by C. H. Patterson; Harrap Ltd., *Man of Everest* by J. R. Ullman; Harrow House Editions Ltd., *Mystery of Migration* by Dr. R.

9

Baker; A. M. Heath & Co. Ltd., and the Literary Estate of the late Alan Watts; Hodder & Stoughton Educational, *The Education of the Whole Man* by L. P. Jacks; William Heinemann Ltd., *They Survived* by C. W. F. Noyce; Dr. N. Humphrey, Bronowski Memorial Lecture 1981; Mrs. Laura Huxley & Chatto & Windus Ltd., *The Perennial Philosophy* by Aldous Huxley; The Hogarth Press Ltd., *The Lost World of Kalahari* and *Yet Being Someone Other* by L. Van Der Post; Houghton Mifflin Company, USA, *The Wilderness World of John Muir* edited by Edwin Teale, and *John of the Mountains* edited by Linnie Marsh Wolfe; R. W. Hodgkin, *Born Curious* (John Wiley publishers); Hutchinson Publishing Group Ltd., *Northface in Winter* by T. Hiebeler; Kodansha International Ltd., *The Unknown Craftsman* by S. Yanagi, adapted by B. Leach; Manjushri Institute, Conishead Priory, Cumbria; Mrs. Meredith, article *Personal Education* by Prof. G. P. Meredith; Methuen London, *Savage Arena* by Joe Tasker; F. Muller Ltd., *Small is Beautiful* by E. F. Schumacher, (Blond & Briggs); Frank Mulville and the Yachting Press Ltd.; The National Children's Bureau; Oxford University Press, *Concise Oxford Dictionary* 7th Ed. 1982; The Rt. Hon. J. Enoch Powell, M.P.; Prentice Hall Inc. USA, *The Beauty of Sport* by B. Lowe; Random House Inc., & Alfred A. Knopf Inc. USA, *The Immense Journey* by L. Eisely; Resurgence magazine; Routledge & Kegan Paul Ltd, *Man for Himself* by Prof. E. Fromm; A. Shiel Associated Ltd., *Shackleton's Boat Journey* by F. A. Worsley, and *The Spirit of the Hills* by F. S. Smythe; Sierra Club Books, *On the Loose* by J. & R. Russell; The Sports Council; Thorsons Publishers Ltd., *Johnathan Livingstone Seagull* by R. Bach (Turnstone Press Ltd.); Times Newspapers Ltd; University of California Press, *Alaskan Wilderness* by R. Marshall; The Viking Press Inc. USA, *The Portable Nietzsche* selected and trans. by W. Kaufman; Westmorland Gazette, *The Central Fells* by A. Wainwright; George Weidenfield & Nicolson Ltd., *Scott of the Antarctic* (Pan Books); Wildwood House Ltd., *The Zen of Running* by F. Rohe; John Wiley & Sons Ltd., *War As I Knew It* by G. S. Patton; John Wyatt, *The Shining Levels* (Penguin Books).

Colin Mortlock

Introduction

There is something delightfully simple in a spontaneous decision to go into the outdoor environment and tackle some form of adventure. It would seem reason enough that it was both enjoyable and satisfying. Certainly as a young rock climber these were my reasons, and I felt no compelling urge to enquire further. Mountaineering as a way of life seemed to be a worthy ideal.

It was with this attitude that in 1960 I first taught secondary schoolboys for a period of three months, in order to earn some money to climb in the Himalayas. As a selfish young man I was convinced that I would never be, and did not want to be, a teacher. I was both surprised and pleased therefore, to find young town lads responding with great enthusiasm to my climbing circuits and commando courses in the gymnasium. Official views of what I was doing, as an unqualified temporary teacher, were somewhat confusing. The local Adviser was appalled by my misuse of equipment, whilst a visiting Inspector was so impressed that he made a film and suggested that I qualify as a teacher! So enjoyable was the physical work with the youngsters that I took them out on gritstone to climb. Their abilities were impressive and matched only by their obvious delight in the sense of freedom and challenge of the activity. Two of them joined me in the Lake District for a week's climbing. It was difficult to believe their performance. At the age of 14 and in shoes, they confidently followed me up many climbs of the Very Severe and Extremely Severe grades. At the end of the week I pointed out the line of a Very Severe route on Castle Rock of Triermain and told them to lead through. I then walked down to the campsite. That week was my first real introduction to the capabilities of the younger generation.

Five years later, in 1965, when leading a schoolboy expedition to Arctic Norway, my awareness of adolescent potential was considerably extended. I had taken a party of 30 boys, sixteen to nineteen

11

years old, from Manchester Grammar School, to a relatively unexplored and rugged mountain area. The specific aims of the expedition were, in the first instance, to climb as many peaks as possible in an area of 100 square miles. The expedition was then to split up and undertake exploratory work ranging from white water canoeing and rock climbing to botanical and geological surveys. The hidden aim of the trip was to find out just how capable were young people in a wilderness environment after a year of progressive training. To this end, the adults with the group were kept to a minimum: myself, my wife (with responsibilities for the scientific work and the catering) and a Doctor. With the expedition working for six weeks, in up to seven small groups, and with an environment that was both hazardous and somewhat remote, there was ample scope for accidents. Perhaps there was an element of luck in that the only such incident was a badly sprained ankle which occurred at Base Camp. What was pleasing was that, despite much bad weather, the practical objectives of the expedition were achieved. This included climbing all the peaks within the specified area. I returned to Britain more than ever convinced about young people's capabilities. They had all been in serious outdoor situations and responded as self-reliant young men.

The next six years at the Woodlands Outdoor Centre in Wales led to an extensive development in my thinking. Unlike the Manchester experience, the Centre catered for a very wide range of intelligence and abilities, as it was used by all the secondary schools from Oxford. Apart from learning that the desire for adventure was likely to be instinctive and that, for educational purposes at least, adventure should be developed as a progressive concept, I found I was deeply impressed by the attitude of most of the adolescents who came for a fortnight of challenge. Not only did they quickly tend to treat the Centre as home during their stay, but they were generally prepared to face up to the problems of fear and discomfort. On winter courses, for example, canoe capsize drill was often a bitterly cold experience, especially without wetsuits! Many other adventure activity groups would also return from days out, both cold and wet, as well as tired and hungry. Determination and courage were characteristic qualities of these young people in these type of situations. Groups also often displayed compassion to any member who might not have much skill but who was prepared to make a great effort. Opting out from a challenge was unusual as it was not traditional within the life of the Centre.

I became so impressed, if not inspired, by their general attitude and by the potential of this type of experience as part of their education, that I eventually called a meeting in North Wales to consider the formation of an Outdoor Association.[1] I particularly hoped that such a body would encourage the development of outdoor adventure 'to meet the needs and abilities of young people'.[2] From this meeting there eventually emerged what has since become The National Association for Outdoor Education.[3] At the same time I found myself writing and lecturing on the need for young people to adventure.

During this period I found considerable opposition to the adventure concept, not least from those who were in responsible positions in Outdoor Education. This opposition was particularly strong amongst the Wardens of Centres, the Advisory Service and the Inspectorate. Somehow the ideas of adventure, fear, physical hardship and discomfort were considered to be inappropriate, and were largely unacceptable as a major aspect of education through the outdoors.[4] In essence my views were seen as narrow, fanatical and dangerous: criticisms that were seldom made face to face. Almost inevitably, and accelerated by the Cairngorm tragedy and fatal incidents in winter in North Wales to young people, the concept of Outdoor Education was developed. By combining outdoor activities with environmental and field studies, educational and academic respectability were achieved. Equally, and very conveniently, fundamental questions concerning adventure, self-reliance and self-development by young people, were largely ignored. It was a subject too dangerous and too radical to bring into prominence.

Ten years of further work with young people and within a community project based in the Lake District[5] strengthened my view both on the broad values of the outdoors as well as of the adventure approach. After the six intensive years working with thirteen to fifteen year olds at the Woodlands Centre, I found my time taken up mainly with boys and girls up to the age of thirteen. The questions in my mind at that time were concerned with whether this young adolescent age group would both enjoy and cope with exciting adventure pursuits such as white water canoeing, rock climbing and survival, in winter as well as summer. If these activities were relevant, then there were serious doubts in my mind concerning possible strength, endurance and exposure problems. There also lurked the more positive thought that there was a possibility that through progressive training, self reliance might be achieved by the age of 12 or 13 – at least in the form of summer expeditions.

With the help of experienced outdoor teachers, who were on my Course at the College,[6] my queries and doubts were answered in a most positive way by the young people involved. I had quite simply underestimated their capabilities. There was no doubt that adventure was relevant to this tender age, that they could acquire considerable levels of skill, and that, not least, they had the courage and determination generally to face up to fatigue and discomfort, cold and fear. In addition, various summer expeditions by them through the hills and down rivers without adults, showed they could work as groups efficiently and be self reliant. The sight of a thirteen year old girl kayaking a grade IV rough river World Championship course with a fleeting smile on her face, remains vividly in my memory. Although the occasion was in a slalom competition, it was nevertheless the epitome of adventure: the journey with a degree of uncertainty with a premium on self reliance.

More importantly, close involvement over five years with some of these youngsters, and their almost daily involvement in the outdoors, has convinced me of the possible deeper values to be gained from such an approach. As young people they seem to be very mature for their age. They tend to accept the need to work hard regularly if they wish to find success in what they do. Their determination is undeniable when they are prepared to kayak regularly early in the morning before school throughout the winter.

Most pleasingly they generally recognise that it is the effort that counts rather than the results, and on weekends away they tend to work and act as a team. Actual success in terms of results, or in representing their country, has not led to arrogance as one might possibly expect. Fears concerning possible deterioration in their academic work at school have also proved groundless. It would seem that they can cope positively with a lifestyle of 'work hard, play hard, and don't mess about'.[7]

Whilst working with this particular group, and with more diverse community groups, has given me a great deal of satisfaction, I could never accept that any form of teaching should replace my own need for adventure. Unlike being at an Outdoor Centre, working from a College gave me the vacation time to expedition, and opportunities were taken both abroad and in Scotland. Most of these experiences were by sea kayak on remote coastlines. Much of my thinking has been inspired from some of these, and earlier adventures in the mountains.

Other experiences have also broadened my views of the values of the self-reliant journey. In particular there were the backpacking and camping expeditions by the family round various islands in Northern Britain.[8] With a wife, who is a keen naturalist, and three young daughters who are diverse in temperament, age and abilities, the expedition challenges were of a different order from my own personal ventures. Instead of the close presence of danger, as with small boat journeys on the sea, there was the challenge of whether the family could find enjoyment and satisfaction from the backpacking and camping in what, at times, was a harsh environment.

Like Sir Edmund Hillary, I found these journeys infinitely rewarding. Back at home there seemed few occasions when the family were all together. Either my wife or I were often out in the evenings and weekends, at meetings, lectures or involved with activities. At the same time, two of the daughters were either involved with homework or their own interests. The contrast with our outdoor journeys was extreme. Having left the car on the mainland, our life became one of simplicity. We would backpack for about eight hours each day, and then camp with evenings on the beach. The essence of these journeys was a return to basic living, with a common objective that required us to work together, play together, and help each other. My awareness respect and love for the family increased, as did my knowledge of the environment. As a family we all felt that we had gained greatly from these experiences.

My work during this period was mainly conerned with running Courses for experienced teachers.[9] On a year's Course it was possible to both share a variety of adventure experiences and to discuss their possible values. With students coming from America, Canada, Australia and New Zealand, as well as from Britain, it was normal to have wide ranging discussions on the outdoor experience. Significantly perhaps, despite the sometimes great diversity of ideas, the basic concept of adventure was never seriously questioned. I suspect that almost anyone who is involved teaching adventure activities to young people, subconsciously and instinctively knows that what he or she is doing has significant value beyond that of learning skills.

The opportunity to explore further the relevance of the values implicit in the wilderness experience came with an invitation to give a lecture at an International Conference in Australia in 1981.[10] I had decided to speak on the state of British Outdoor Education and it seemed necessary to take a careful look at the state of Western Society and its education systems as essential background. The evidence I found was very disturbing and seemed to underline the essential need for adventure as a central part of the education of young people. As Solzenitsyn found, Western Society is dominated by a lack of courage and ego-centred trivia.[11] It defines progress as increased security and a greater ease of living, and by an increase in the Gross National Product. If, as would seem reasonable, mankind is searching for happiness, then this type of 'progressive' society is obviously in very serious difficulties. Figures for suicide rates, mental illness, drug abuse, divorce, crime and vandalism are both very high and increasing throughout Western Society. The time honoured human qualities so essential in any civilization are largely ignored, unless they are convenient, or increase the power or status of the people or country involved. Instead of integrity, dishonesty and deceit are rampant throughout all layers of society.[12] Instead of humility, arrogance is commonplace. Instead of self-reliance, the Welfare State approach has led to a great deal of irresponsibility. It is normal for people to evade responsibility for their actions if at all possible. It is convenient to pass the responsibility either on to someone else, or to some committee. In a similar way, emphasis on individual freedom has led to an attitude of 'I'm alright Jack', and an evasion of responsibilities as a member of society. Selfishness and apathy concerning the future of mankind are typical attitudes.

These disturbing trends of modern man and 'the nuclear age' are of course unacceptable to many people. If one looks beyond government and multi-national corporations, and into the lives of many individuals, then one will find the universal values, or at least some of them, are still very much in evidence. As a society Britain, for example, still places courage as something of special importance. Compassion and unselfishness too are reflected in the myriad of caring and helping organisations. There are also many bodies concerned with the protection of the natural environment and its wildlife.

An increasing number of people have rejected the trend of modern materialism and, in a variety of ways, developed alternative lifestyles and ideals more attuned to men as part of nature. This 'New Age' movement[13] is beginning to attract media attention in much the same way as the Green movement in Europe.[14]

Whilst it is difficult not to be highly encouraged both by the amount and extent of voluntary work, and the increase in alternative lifestyles, it does seem however, that in practice, they are almost totally peripheral to the political juggernauts that ruthlessly exploit both the earth and less fortunate human beings. None of the major political parties, in terms of their actions, appear to be prepared radically to change direction away from the aims of a higher standard of living.

The same comment can be made generally about the education system, which will always tend to reflect the aims of the society. Increased security and ease of living by way of examination 'success' is still the tradition, despite at least 20 years of attempts to change this system. The result can be seen in most secondary school classrooms around the country: boredom and restlessness rather than vitality and enthusiasm. When the bell goes for the end of the school, there tends to be a swift and joyous exodus. Education has finished for the day and the adolescent can relax and really live! And then of course for many, there is the endless homework – usually a tedious chore that is often done with resentment and without enthusiasm.

The effect of this traditional approach to secondary education is not only to stunt the growth of many young people but, in their eyes at least, to brand a majority of them as academic failures. Many of them know that in practice, school is often only concerned with the numbers of examination passes. Nothing else appears to matter. The resultant damage to such adolescents must be enormous. Not only do they tend to lack self confidence and vitality, but they will tend to treat any form of education in later life with contempt.

As recognised by many scientists and philosophers, the world is now at a crisis point in its history. The greed of selfish materialism by the advanced nations, has led to huge problems both within those societies, and in terms of providing sufficient resources for the health and well-being of the entire human race. If it is accepted that there is a duty to try and safeguard the happiness and well-being of the entire human race, then it is obvious that there must be a radical change of attitude by modern societies. Almost from the dawn of history, outstanding men and women have shown the way by the qualities they have displayed. These include COURAGE: COMPASSION: DETERMINATION: INTEGRITY: HUMILITY and SELF RELIANCE. Such qualities, and associated ones, should be openly recognised within society as of supreme importance, and way beyond those of physical or intellectual excellence, important though these are in themselves.

At the same time as endorsing the value of these qualities, modern man must avoid at all costs, the temptation to be greedy and selfish. All his actions should be based within the following broad framework:–

To try and develop, to the best of his ability,

AN AWARENESS OF, RESPECT FOR, AND LOVE OF SELF balanced against

AN AWARENESS OF, RESPECT FOR, AND LOVE OF OTHERS balanced against

AN AWARENESS OF, RESPECT FOR, AND LOVE OF THE ENVIRONMENT

This means, in effect that modern man will reject the arrogant concept that he can conquer Nature. Instead, he will accept not only that he is part of Nature, but that, as its supposedly most advanced form of life, he has a huge responsibility for the happiness and well-being of ALL forms of life.

The great message of twentieth century biology is that all human life, and indeed all life, has an essential unity; and that all forms of life share a common ancestry, and use the same genetic code. In the same way, all human beings have common needs – for food, shelter, security creative self-expression, and the freedom to explore ideas. If the human species is to continue, then each individual needs to face up to the tremendous problems of the modern world, and to act according to his conscience. Hope and optimism can give us the strength of mind, along with the acceptance that our earth, divided against itself, cannot stand; and that war is not the answer. A world without frontiers must be the aim of modern man. First, however, he must learn to cross the frontiers of his own mind and discover something of his enormous potential for constructive and expanding activities rather than self destruction. My experiences have led me to believe that the adventurous and self-reliant journey in the natural environment, can provide him with an opportunity to discover himself.

CHAPTER 1

Adventure

To adventure in the natural environment is consciously to take up a challenge that will demand the best of our capabilities – physically, mentally and emotionally. It is a state of mind that will initially accept unpleasant feelings of fear, uncertainty and discomfort, and the need for luck, because we instinctively know that, if we are successful, these will be counterbalanced by opposite feelings of exhilaration and joy. This journey with a degree of uncertainty in the 'University of the Wilderness' may be of any length in terms of distance or time; in any dimension – above, on or below ground or water.

It may be climbing up a ten foot slab covered with large holds or the biggest and steepest rock face in the world.

It may be canoeing down the easiest or hardest rapid in the world, or the shortest or longest river.

It may be sailing on a lake or across an ocean.

In all cases you, the person in the situation, are being challenged to the best of your abilities. If you have given of your genuine best, and either overcome the challenge or retreated with dignity through skill and experience rather than luck alone, then you have had one of the greatest experiences of your life. You have had a 'peak experience' with feelings almost indescribable and beyond those common to normal and routine living. Ultimately life is about feelings, those that are concerned with the joy of living, rather than the anxieties of modern existence.

****

It is your first rock climb. You are a complete beginner, and the older you are, the more likely that you have doubts and inhibitions (such is the paradox of maturation!). The instructor has briefed you and the rest of the group on the climbing communication calls and safety arrangements. Your helmet has been adjusted and you are tied on to the blunt end of the rope.* The instructor quickly leads up the 100 foot rock face making it look easy, belays at the top, and calls down for you to begin climbing. The others wish you luck as you tentatively start up the rock. Your boots, and movements generally, feel clumsy, but as the holds appear, which seemed invisible from below, you gradually gain both height and confidence. At 40 feet the rock becomes more difficult, and you only get up the next section because the instructor both encourages you and explains how to use the holds. You manage quite well, but immediate enjoyment is somewhat spoilt by the feeling that this is becoming serious – the rope looks incredibly thin, and those jagged and menacing boulders at the foot of the climb look a long way down.

At 80 feet you reach a crisis point. The rock steepens. You can't see any good handholds above and your arms are feeling tired. If you could, you'd stop the experience right now, and go back to horizontal living. Your mind is a jumble of thoughts: 'What if I ask for slack and climb back down? But that would mean reversing that bit at 40 foot and I might fall off. And anyway what would my mates below say? It's alright for them, they're not up here. Still, they'll have their turn!' You listen to the instructor telling you how to do the next few moves and that you should relax because you're quite safe. 'Safe! I don't feel safe and anyway it's alright for him, he's a climber'. You still can't see how to do the next section and you feel anger. 'Why am I doing this? It's crazy. I'll just stop here and he can rescue me.'

The battle rages within you. You look again at the problem. 'Yes, maybe if I move up left on that hold, I can reach this good hold he's talking about'. Your positive thoughts just win out; you keep your fear in check (just!), and with a tense 'tight rope!' you start moving upwards. Almost unbelievably the 'thank God' hold arrives, the crisis point vanishes, and soon you arrive on the top – shattered, amazed, overjoyed and exhilarated all in one crowded moment. The ground and your friends look a long way down, but now the distance doesn't feel hostile. You feel great and sit back to enjoy watching the rest climb. You are aware that the view from the top is superb.

As the others climb, you notice their reactions. Some find the

---

*The blunt end refers to the end of the rope used by those who follow up a rock climb. The leader used the sharp end of the rope. The different terminology for the rope ends is concerned with the implications of falling off.

whole climb easy, and don't appear to have experienced your exhilaration. Others find parts of the climb so hard that when they finally reach the top, they appear more relieved than exhilarated. One lad falls off, is held on the rope, and then eventually retreats to the ground. He doesn't seem happy at all with his climbing experience.

The next day you can go canoeing. You've been told that the instructor is a fanatical white water canoeist, who has been on TV. As you're not keen on cold water, you're apprehensive even at breakfast time. This is considerably increased when he takes the group to a rapid on a river, and says the group will canoe down the rapid. 'He must be mad – we've never canoed before – and those waves are all white and the current looks really fast'. Again, reluctantly, but somehow excited, you put on a crash helmet and buoyancy aid and listen intently on what to do, especially if you capsize. Thankfully you're not the first one to go and you note, with relief, that the two before you seem to be smiling when they reached the pool at the foot of the rapid, and they didn't capsize!

You sit in your canoe and seem to be a tight fit. Dismal thoughts well up about, 'What if I capsize and can't get out?' You're very tense as you push off – this isn't enjoyable and the noise of the rapid sounds horrid. You haven't time to think much – you're moving down swiftly and spray is hitting you in the face. There's a sudden and sickening jolt, the canoe tips, and in a flash you're upside down and terrified – trapped, and the water is unbelievably cold. You fight to get out, but your legs are stuck in the boat. Through your panic, you remember dimly, instructions about dog paddling to get your nose above the water to breathe. As you do this, your legs come free and you're floating down the river. The instructor is by you. You grab the end of his boat and are soon at the bank – soaking wet, cold and, above all, relieved that you're still alive. No enjoyment, no exhilaration, just relief and acute discomfort from the cold. You note that others who capsize have similar reactions, whilst others who don't, obviously seem to have really enjoyed the experience. One lad, who has canoed before, doesn't seem affected in any way by the experience, although he obviously enjoys the capsizes of the others.

In the afternoon, after a hot shower, you canoe on flat water. You learn some of the skills of boat handling, and manage not to capsize again. You are pleased with what you have learnt, but somehow the session wasn't as exciting and certainly didn't compare with rock climbing.

****

Twenty years of putting people of all ages in these adventure situations, in a wide variety of activities, and noting their reactions and comments, has led me to believe that there are four broad stages discernible in any outdoor journey. The person involved, whether he is a beginner or the most experienced of performers, would seem to be in one of these stages at any particular moment on a journey:

STAGE ONE: PLAY
This is the level in the activity in which the person is working or playing considerably below his normal abilities. He has minimal involvement, therefore, in terms of emotion, skills, mental control and concentration. Fear of physical harm is absent. His response to this level of activity will range from 'pleasant' and 'fun' to 'boring' and a 'waste of time'.

STAGE TWO: ADVENTURE
The person feels in control of the situation, but is using his experience and abilities to overcome a technical problem. Fear of physical harm is virtually absent, because the person is in control. If fear does exist, it lurks beneath the surface, because although he knows he is in control, he may still be in a potentially dangerous, or strange, environment.

An adult deliberately sets himself a problem as a personal challenge which with effort, and barring incidents, he feels he can overcome with satisfaction. He has deliberately not pitched his challenge too low to the 'playing' stage, because he instinctively knows it will bring minimal reward. On the other hand he has deliberately not set his challenge too near his personal limitations. He knows that to do this, is to court the likelihood of physical harm should a mistake ensue or bad luck intervene.

In pupil terms, this is the level where the teacher tends to work in SKILLS LEARNING. The pupil can apply himself, as the problem set is a challenge to his technical abilities in particular. He is not disturbed by feelings of boredom and lack of involvement, nor by the psychological stress of the next stage.

This stage is of crucial importance as preparation for any demanding journey.

STAGE THREE: FRONTIER ADVENTURE

This is the stage beyond, and often just beyond, stage II. The person has fear of physical harm, or physical or psychological stress, and no longer feels complete master of the situation. He feels, however, that he can, with considerable effort on his part, and given luck, overcome the situation without accident. He accepts that his skills are about to be tested. He is conscious of a definite degree of uncertainty as to the outcome, and feels, as it were, poised on a knife edge between success and failure. If he succeeds, he has experienced what I would term 'frontier adventure'. He has found himself in a situation which becomes firmly etched upon his mind – perhaps forever. He has feelings of satisfaction, if not elation, about the result. The degree of satisfaction and pride is proportional to the scale and intensity of the experience.

STAGE FOUR: MISADVENTURE

This is the final stage – when the challenge is in any way beyond the control of the person. In ultimate form the result is death, but between death and serious injuries on the one hand and frontier adventure on the other, there are various degrees of both physical and psychological damage. It is possible and indeed not infrequent in practice to experience misadventure without any form of physical injury. In mild examples, the reaction will be one of immediate dissatisfaction and self-rebuke, because the person has been in an adventure situation in which he has acquitted himself badly. The classic case of this type is the person trying, or being made to try, something that involves a degree of technical skill, or degree of control over his fear, that is beyond his abilities. Paradoxically in many mild cases of stage IV, the learning experience may be of great value to the participant. Fear, however, can easily be of an extreme nature in misadventure. Where it leads to panic and terror it is unjustifiable in educational terms.

In the examples given at the start of the chapter, the climbing experience would be stage I for the instructor, stage III for those who had to battle up the climb, and who reacted with immediate feelings of 'that was great'; stage IV for the person who fell off and retreated; and stage I and II for those who got up easily, and weren't worried by the height. In the canoeing example in the morning session, those who capsized were very likely to be in stage IV during the capsize; stage II or III if they were 'gripped up', but managed successfully; and stage I for the lad who had done it all before. The afternoon session was likely to have been mainly stage II with stage IV in first time capsizes.

There are some important general comments to be made about the stages of adventure:

– Each stage is extremely broad, especially stage III
– On a journey or during an experience, a person may go through several or all the stages, perhaps several times. The order of the stages will depend upon when the problems occur during the journey.
– The 'Play' Stage (I) is concerned with minimal feelings and involvement.
– The Adventure Stage (II) is concerned with positive and satisfying human feelings progressing in intensity to the peak experiences of the Frontier Adventure Stage (III). The positive feelings of stage II, and especially stage III, are of the type that make life feel worth living, and are potentially available to almost anyone.
– The Misadventure Stage (IV) is concerned with immediate negative and disruptive feelings.

CHAPTER 2

Stage II – Skills Learning and Adventure

In the 'first adventure' examples of the preceding chapter, it will be noted that the performers were more or less complete beginners, and yet were able to experience the peak experience feelings of stage III. This was providing that the challenge made big demands on them, which they were able to handle – both in psychological and in physical terms.

The 'perfect' beginner session by an instructor will ensure that all the group experience stage III, and avoid both the boredom of stage I, and the negative reactions likely from stage IV. The instructor who can do this deserves respect, for he may well need a whole range of different challenges within each activity in order to meet the requirements of each individual adventure threshold – especially in a mixed ability group, as is common in Centre work. He may also have time and the environment working against him. In introductory abseiling, for example, one group member may need a 150 foot free abseil to reach stage III, whilst another may find a 10 foot slab abseil evokes the same feelings. Similarly, certain activities are particularly difficult in this respect. Hill walking, being a group activity and featuring movement that youngsters had done since very young, can be a considerable problem. A radical approach, such as carefully selected solo or small group unaccompanied walks, may be necessary. It may be worth noting that, without adults present, a cow in a field, or climbing over a gate, can be stage III for some youngsters.

However, no matter how difficult provision of stage III might be, it is essential to try and provide it for each beginner as an introduction. Failure to do so can have the following result:
– If the introduction is stage I, then it may convince him that the particular activity is no more adventurous than football or hockey.
– If the introduction is stage II, it may convince him that the

25

activity is not particularly exciting.

– If the introduction is stage IV, then it may convince him that the activity is too frightening for him, and never to be repeated.

At this introductory level, it is acceptable for the beginner to experience stage III because the danger is 'apparent' rather than real. In the rock climb, for example, the instructor has selected a suitable climb and area where, even if the beginner falls off, he is safely held on the rope. Similarly in the canoeing situation, the capsize should at worst be only an unpleasant experience without any chance of drowning. There is no justification whatsoever for real danger situation with beginners. Paradoxically, however, neither is there any justification for stopping development by a beginner who, having had a stage III introduction, decides he wants to pursue that activity. Indeed there is a strong case for all youngsters to have to do some form of self-reliant journey as a CENTRAL part of their education.

To stop at the introductory stage is to say that the realities of life are to be avoided. The leaders of western society may aim for greater security and greater ease of living, but there can be no doubt that modern society is full of dangers – many of them are unnatural, insidious and the direct result of a modern lifestyle. Young people need to be equipped to meet such dangers such as mental illness, neuroticism, alcoholism, drug abuse, as well as the likely long term consequences of a slothful existence. They need to have faced up to natural dangers and to have developed sufficient maturity, self-reliance and a set of positive human values that will stand them in good stead in the serious problems they are likely to face in adult life. The skills learning commitment of stage II, and the peak experiences of frontier adventure can make a vital contribution in this direction. The Duke of Edinburgh Award Expedition Scheme, and the Outward Bound concept, can be seen as positive steps in the right direction although both fall short in providing the range and level of activities that really meet the needs and abilities of many of the younger generation.

Once the young person, or any beginner, has found the adventure journey of his choice, then he needs to set his sights on both short and long term goals, If it is climbing, then the short term goals could be to learn competently to lead one pitch rock climbs that will challenge his capabilities, but which can be protected; and secondly to follow multi-pitch climbs in the major rock areas of Britain. His long term goals could be climbing with his peers in the Alps, and, ultimately, expeditions to the more remote mountain ranges of the world.

In a similar way the canoeist can aim, in the short term, to be efficient on white water river journeys in Britain – journeys which will tax his abilities. In the long term he can aim to kayak the bigger and more serious rivers of the Alps, and ultimately, perhaps to expedition down rivers in the Andes or Himalayas. Alternatively he may opt to go in for rough water competition.

In both and similar examples from other types of adventure, the aims are to become self-reliant in the execution of journeys which consistently and progressively tax the performer in proportion to his levels of experience and ability. This process can and should continue to the point where the most experienced and most capable humans tackle the hardest and most dangerous problems within each adventure activity. Society rightly applauds the ultimate adventurers and is deeply saddened when, inevitably, some do not return. Indeed, one might be tempted to note that the great adventure journeys of mankind – both those that have succeeded and those that have failed – have made a very significant contribution towards inspiring people to realise the magnificent potential of the human being.

To return, however, to our committed beginner. He, or she, has to spend a great deal of time learning all the relevant skills, within the context of stage II, as preparation for stage III peak experiences. Deciding which are the relevant skills, and the learning of them, is highly complex, and yet crucially important if the performer is to perform at maximum capability levels efficiently and safely. There can be little doubt, however, that unless all the relevant skills are learnt efficiently, and that means performing them in stress situations – then the results are most likely to be misadventure rather than a peak experience. Once it is realised that situations can, and do, occur which seek out the weaknesses in the skills armoury of the performer, and that the strength of a chain is in its weakest link, then learning all the skills, and especially those in which one is weak, becomes essential.

Two personal examples might illustrate the point. As a climber who was very fit and climbing at Exceptionally Severe standard I tackled what was then a Hard Very Severe route in North Wales.[1] It should have been an adventure experience well within my capabilities. In practice, it became a very frightening stage IV and taught me an obvious lesson, luckily without the injuries I deserved.

The main part of the climb was a 120 foot vertical corner requiring hand jam techniques. I couldn't hand jam efficiently, had always disliked it (because I was no good at it), and was used to laybacking as an alternative, as I was fairly strong. Any climber knows that the latter technique is very strenuous, whilst jamming tends to be less strenuous and, crucially, often allows 'resting'. This gives the balance necessary to place running belays, thereby safeguarding against possible falls. As I climbed up I attempted to jam, rest, and place protection. Each time I did so I felt insecure, felt I was losing strength, and thus decided to move on by laybacking, in the hope of less strenuous resting positions. I didn't find them, and as I moved further and further up the corner, I realised that I had no protection and was rapidly running out of strength. My fears drastically increased into a stage IV situation, and it became a question of whether I could 'solo' sufficiently quickly up the top half of the corner, before I fell off through exhaustion. That I just managed to do so was in no way due to skill, but to luck and determination. I deserved to fall off because I lacked an essential skill for that type of climb.

The other example concerned canoeing when, as a comparative beginner, I took an even less experienced friend and tackled a gorge in central Wales, in very high flood.[2] Unbeknown to us a highly experienced group who knew the river well and whom we passed on the road to the gorge, had decided it was impossible if not suicidal! Once round the first bend of the river, we were into the foaming gorge and totally committed. Just in control, and very much into stage III, I was eventually hit by a massive side shoot of water, which turned me over. As I went over, I knew that I had to eskimo roll. Failure to have done so would have greatly increased possibilities of drowning as the river went down through the trees and stoppers, and I would have been entirely at the dictates of the river. Unfortunately, although my rolling in a swimming pool was efficient, it was very unpractised in rough rivers. Luckily I just managed to roll – in time to see my friend capsized by the same piece of water. He came out of his boat, and I managed to rescue him, although we finally located his boat another mile downstream. Again my lack of a particular technical skill: efficient rough river rolling – which should have been practised in safe situations – had not only nearly led to disaster for me, but could also have placed my friend, who was younger and for whom I felt responsibility, in a similar situation.

In both these examples I made serious errors of judgement which produced unjustifiably dangerous situations, unjustifiable because escape from them was more a matter of luck rather than skill. Certainly the reactions were those of relief, rather than satisfaction.

The skills required for any self-reliant adventurous journey can be roughly categorized into four broad sections:

TECHNICAL SKILLS
(i)   as required by each activity in terms of efficient movement and resting – and particularly concerned with balance and rhythm,
(ii) the efficient use of relevant equipment to aid movement and resting and to be used for emergency situations.

FITNESS SKILLS
(i)   the specific fitness demanded by a particular activity,
(ii) general cardio-circulatory fitness,
(iii) body conditioning to the relevant stress environment.

HUMAN SKILLS
Development of a very positive attitude to all aspects of the skills learning, including:
(i)   Determination, self-confidence, patience, concentration, self-analysis,
(ii) self-reliance,
(iii) the ability to both follow and lead efficiently.

ENVIRONMENTAL SKILLS
The development of awareness of the qualities and hazards of any specific environment.

There is no easy road to the acquisition of all these skills, and almost inevitably some skills are likely to be comparatively weak. The gifted teacher will be able to help the learner, particularly in those areas of weakness. Basically the aim is to develop and hone all the skills as tools required for the stage III journey. Constant repetition in progressively more demanding situations is essential. At all times, however, there should be a safety framework for the learner. Failure to provide it, will mean the learner will learn very inefficiently because he is unduly anxious.

The approach of the learner is critical at all stages. In simple terms, if he is tense, then he will neither perform nor learn efficiently. This tenseness may even be subconscious. In other

29

words he may feel he is relaxed in the learning situation, but in practice his poor performance is due to subconsciously being tense. The modern development of organisations, like 'The Inner Game'[3] and the 'Sporting Bodymind'[4] seem specifically aimed at ensuring that learners of all degrees of competence, are genuinely relaxed in order that they may develop skills and perform as efficiently as possible. The approach of these organisations had highlighted a critical problem in learning, and not least in adventure activities, where inevitably, at times, there is a high degree of emotional stress.

To give an example, it is not uncommon to find beginner canoeists unable to grasp the principles of basic boat handling on white water. The techniques required can be easily understood but the learner constantly capsizes. Sometimes this is simply because the learner is subconsciously tense, although he says he is not worried about capsizing. An approach that can be dramatically effective in such a situation is to forget all thoughts of developing the technical skills, and allow the learner to capsize as often as he likes. Providing he has a high determination to learn, then eventually (and it may take several sessions) his body will become relaxed in that environment whether above or below the surface. Once this has been achieved, then the technical skills can often be rapidly developed. The paradox of life emerges again, in that the learner who capsizes the most in initial sessions could well eventually become a star performer. The art of relaxing and yet concentrating at the same time is vital not only for skills development, but for when those skills are tested on an adventurous journey.

The whole process of skills learning, which must start from a base of psychological relaxation, has as its aim, to be 'at one' with the challenging environment, and to flow with it. The act of climbing, canoeing, sailing, and so on, should become as fluent as walking down a road. A very great deal of progressive practice is necessary, and ideally, (and at the risk of being called a fanatic!) almost daily practice in some aspect of the skills may be necessary, if the performer is to reach anything like his true potential. The growth in popularity of climbing walls, for example, has led to startling improvements in performance because of the ease of access of the facility for many climbers.

Although hard work is unavoidable if real progress is to be made, it should be obvious that enjoyment and satisfaction are essential during the learning process – at least for most of the time!

Before moving on to Stage III, Frontier Adventure, and the consequent testing of the acquired skills, it is necessary to look at safety.

CHAPTER 3

Safety

'A SHIP IN HARBOUR IS SAFE,
but that is not what ships are for'[1]

THE FRAMEWORK
The first consideration of the teacher is to ensure that his pupils are as free as possible from physical or psychological harm during the activity. If an accident happens, he has to be sure that he can face himself, the pupil, or the parents, or the coroner, by knowing that he was justified in being in that place at that time, and that he had taken all sensible precautions for that journey.

Those responsible for Outdoor Pursuits must be able to decide whether a particular situation is basically SAFE or DANGEROUS. If it is the latter, then distinction must be made between the two factors that have made it dangerous:
FACTOR ONE: SUBJECTIVE DANGER
FACTOR TWO: OBJECTIVE DANGER

Subjective danger is that potentially under the control of the human being, such as the correct choice and use of equipment needed, and the correct selection of the journey to meet the requirements of the party in terms of safety.

Objective danger is that over which the human being has no control e.g. avalanches, blizzards, floods, storms, exposed situations.

Work with young people, who are beginners, will be in the subjective danger sector. In effect this should mean that, although they may feel the journey or experience is dangerous, in reality there should be a minimum of danger because the instructor has taken all the appropriate safety precautions. These may be termed situations of apparent danger. As the beginner becomes more experienced and self reliant, the challenges can justifiably contain an increasing amount of objective danger. No particular age can be recommended at which a young person should be allowed to take on journeys containing objective dangers. Indeed, adolescents who have been properly and progressively trained are already leading

Danger Diagram

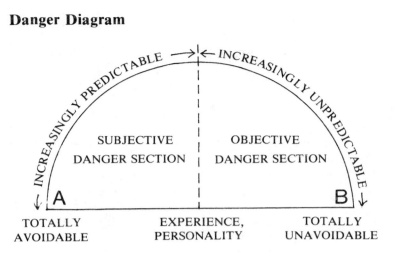

With reference to the diagram, beginners will be working at the left end of the base line AB. Committed experts will be taking on the challenges at the right end of the base line.

exposed and serious rock climbs, and tackling flooded white water rivers.

It is true that no amount of expertise can hide the fact that Outdoor Pursuits are potentially dangerous and accidents can happen to anyone. Human frailty apart, there is always a place for both bad and good luck. There is no doubt, however, that most accidents are the result of subjective danger, including the taking of a school party into an unjustifiable situation of objective danger. Most accidents, therefore, are avoidable.

Despite its fundamental importance, safety is not the reason for taking part in Outdoor Pursuits. Safety is the essential framework.[2] Without proper concern for it, this form of education is untenable.

GENERAL COMMENTS

Of all the aspects of Adventure Education, the subject of safety and young people is the most emotive and contentious. In many countries in the western world, young people are simply not allowed to become self-reliant on adventurous journeys as part of their education. Britain is probably an exception in that it does allow this type of education, albeit in a somewhat negative manner, with its masses of safety rules, regulations and certificates.

In essence the problem revolves around serious accidents to young people in adventure situations. Unless young people are banned from such journeys, it is inevitable that there will be accidents, because human beings are not perfect, and because of the unpredictability of Nature. Even the most experienced of adventurers recognise the need for luck. Risk is as basic to adventure as competition is to sport, but the stakes are normally higher. The question becomes, what level of risk is acceptable for a young person? I have already mentioned that for beginners there should be virtually no real danger. This is common sense, and relevant to any age. Herein perhaps lies the way forward to solving this difficult question. The level of risk should depend entirely upon the competence and experience of the performer, rather than the artificial device of imposed age limits. The latter approach, as used by the Duke of Edinburgh Award Scheme, for example, where boys and girls may not start their bronze expeditions until they are fourteen, is wrong. In the same way, Local Education Authorities that use their Outdoor Centres primarily for the thirteen to fifteen age range, rather than younger age groups, is probably a mistaken policy.

There is a marked tendency in modern society for adults to consistently underrate and under-value the general capabilities of the young generation. The tendency may well be, at least in part, for reasons of convenience. Whatever the reasons, young people in the seven to twelve year old age range, for example, can be surprisingly capable. It also happens to be the ideal age to acquire many of the outdoor skills. In working with this age range, I have been very impressed, to such an extent that I believe that the development of Outdoor Pursuits in this country has been severely handicapped by concentration on the 13 to 16 age range.

First, there can be little doubt that the seven to eleven year olds are ideally suited to acquiring many of the technical skills. Compared to older adolescents, they are usually uninhibited and their sense of balance tends to be better. Secondly, qualities of attentive listening, determination, perseverance, and the ability to put up with fear and discomfort, can also easily compare favourably with older age groups. Indeed these type of necessary human qualities may well be more a characteristic or otherwise of a particular person, rather than a particular age group. Thirdly, the top end of this age range – the 11 to 12 year olds – can learn to work efficiently together to the point where they can undertake self-reliant expeditions in hazardous environments, over a period of days.

Society, of course, would want hard evidence before it would accept self reliant journeys by such young people. Even then it would be highly unlikely that it would be allowed as a formal part of education. Indeed many educational organisations are still unhappy about 16 year olds leading rock climbs, or canoeing and sailing expeditions. I cannot provide much hard evidence but I feel strongly that all the signs are evident that the 11 to 12 year olds, suitably trained, can be self reliant in almost any adventure type of activity. Here are some of the indications:

ROCK CLIMBING: 12 year old boys and younger have been soloing gritstone climbs up to Hard Very Severe standards. Youngsters of similar age have been leading adults on multi-pitch climbs in Wales and the Lakes up to Extremely Severe standards. Sixteen year olds climb together in the same areas up to the same standards.

MOUNTAINEERING: School expeditions to the Himalayas and other mountain ranges, have included peaks climbed without adults.

HILL WALKING: 11 and 12 year olds have completed self-reliant expeditions in the Lakeland fells in poor weather in summer. (The progress of these groups was carefully monitored by teachers who kept out of sight of the youngsters during their journey.)

CANOEING: Three years ago I had a group of 10 boys and girls aged 12 to 13 years, who completed a 100 mile river expedition carrying all their food and equipment. This group had been canoeing for two years and managed the expedition without problems, despite bad weather and the river in spate. Six of this group of local youngsters are now at international level in slalom and white water racing, not because they have exceptional ability, but rather because they have had the opportunities and have worked very hard. They take winter canoeing and grade IV rough water in their stride.

A glance at the sporting achievements of this group also indicates the tremendous potential of their generation – not just in skills acquisition – but in terms of human skills such as determination and surprisingly perhaps, endurance. Marathons have been run by as young as 9 year olds; a 12 year old has swum the Channel; another has completed the Haute Route on ski; 16 year olds have qualified as glider pilots and have sailed solo round the world. These are surely the ideal type of experiences we would want young people to have, if they are ready for them. This is particularly true if young men are expected to be sufficiently mature to fight for their country, as happened in the Falklands War.

The reader may well be critical of my encouragement of such a young age group being involved in genuinely dangerous journeys. Without the experience of the last five years I would not have put forward this view. During these years I have seen local youngsters mature remarkably as a result of adventure experiences, and this includes one of my own daughters. There have been times when I have felt an almost intolerable degree of stress, because I have been responsible for the group, the river has been in a dangerous condition, and I could not control either the performance of the youngsters in the situation, or the river. At such times I have had to take an optimistic view, as well as mentally rehearse all the emergency actions. The young people concerned have been ready for the particular experience, they knew the dangers, as did their parents. In such circumstances, it is easier to cancel the journey but that would be the wrong decision.

The one occasion where I felt the danger to be totally unacceptable was unexpected. It happened at a Division III slalom event in Northern England, where the river was in full spate and the rescue facility was inadequate. A 15 year old girl became stuck in her kayak in a stopper* in the centre of the river, without any form of rescue available.** That she didn't drown was due to luck. In competitions of this kind, of course, such situations should never arise. That it did was another reminder that serious situations can, and do, occur at unexpected times.

In summary, concerning safety, self-reliant adventurous journeys should be accepted for any age group, in any activity, providing that:

(i)   they have been properly trained by someone who is suitably experienced, and who is aware that accidents can happen anytime.

(ii) all those concerned with the intended journey are aware of the

* the stationary wave at the foot of a fall in the river bed.
** the canoeist on rescue duty was 50 metres downstream rescuing the previous competitor. Frogmen rescuers were not provided and the incident was about 20 metres away from the nearest river bank.

dangers and their implications (This must include the youngsters themselves, their parents, and the officials of any organisation involved.

At the same time those involved should know that society in general and its leaders, are concerned with increased security and ease of living. In other words there is a general attitude of 'If there is an accident then in no way do I accept the responsibility.' In part this is due to the anxiety caused by a media cult which makes massive headlines out of incidents to the young in the outdoors. Finally, that even if a young person is ready for serious adventure, then the parents are understandably under serious pressure. They, hopefully, want to allow the youngsters to participate, but like everyone else they do not want accidents. Providing there is a general awareness of what is involved, courage perhaps is an appropriate word in such circumstances. Faint-hearted bureaucrats who are totally removed from the outdoor experience, and who have no concept of its value in helping young people grow up, should have no powers in these matters.

CHAPTER 4

Frontier Adventure

The peak experience of stage III is rather like going through a door into another world, which is altogether more magnificent and more indescribable than normal living. Once through that door, other doors beckon, if you have the key to them. Peak experience – living on the edge of life – and understanding the process – may well hold some of the answers to the riddle of human existence. Feelings of freedom and wonder, happiness and exhilaration, are typical reactions. Opposite feelings, if one is still alive, are typical reactions if one goes over the edge into stage IV. As with everything else, the human being is subject to the balance of Nature.

The 'feeling great' reaction of stage III is, in essence, due to overcoming a challenge that had seemed almost impossible. As one's experience and skill develops, one realizes that life is, or should be, a succession of peaks and hollows, and that each peak surmounted must be followed by a higher or more difficult peak. The spectrum of stage III is extremely broad, and in terms of human potential, very exciting. The problems, however, in staying on the adventure road, and tackling increasingly more difficult challenges, are innumerable. The way forward is not always obvious, and can be frustrating.

In the first instance, there is the problem of the approach of the performer in his first frontier adventure. He may have worked hard in his stage II skills learning, and feels ready to take on the challenge. He tackles the problem prepared to fight his way through. Although he may well have seen experts in action, he probably has not noticed that, almost regardless of their particular activity, they seem to make even hard challenges look easy – they seem to have great rhythm, and to flow rather than fight. Even if he has noted their rhythm and grace, he will likely not feel that it is, in any way, relevant to him as a comparative novice. Yet his approach is critical.

If he fights the challenge, then he is likely to be tense – almost by definition. Tenseness is not conducive to rhythmic and efficient performance. Instead of fighting he needs to develop the 'relaxed concentration' of the expert. In its truest sense, this type of concentration will only usually come after years of hard work and awareness. It is the hallmark of the master craftsman, or expert, in anything. It will help the beginner, however, if he can realize that his performance is dependent on his emotions and mental powers, as well as his technical and physical abilities. All need to be working together with a quiet self-confidence, if he is both to perform efficiently and feel 'great' as a result. Pure relief after a challenge is an indication of going too far, taking on something too difficult, where luck has played an undue part – a mild stage IV situation rather than a peak experience.

In the second instance, there is the problem of finding the appropriate stage III situation for the experience of the person. Although one can decide approximately what that challenge should be, the outdoors cannot be regulated to suit the specific requirements of the individual. If I want a particular type of vehicle then it is likely I can find it. If I want a particular level of adventure in a particular activity, then this can be really difficult. Rock climbing is probably one of the easiest activities in which to find a suitable level, but even here there can be problems. Quite apart from the weather playing havoc with the condition of climbs, there are problems with whether the grading of the climb suits your individual abilities. A low grade route can sometimes appear much harder because it is not your style of climbing, and vice-versa. Similarly the question of protection arises. The guidebook description may not be helpful in this respect. Even when it is helpful, there may still be problems of whether you are carrying the appropriate equipment; whether you can find the places in which to use it; and whether you have the skill to rest sufficiently to set it up properly.

Other adventure activities can be worse by a significant degree. In canoeing on white water rivers, for example, a single rapid can vary between easy and safe to very difficult and dangerous – dependent on the level of the water. Between the two, there can be a whole range of difficulties according to river level. And contrary to what might be expected, sometimes, both difficulty and danger can increase with a decrease in water. Similarly an easy grade I river may become lethal in spate, particularly for the unwary.

In the third instance, there is the problem of finding one's limit. It very often seems to have been reached quickly! It might be true to say that the great explorers and adventurers are people who have gone well beyond what they thought were their limitations; that they are people who are unusual in the sense that they have persevered when most people would have given up. It is far too easy to accept what appear to be our limitations. If the will is strong enough, then those limitations can often be overcome. For example, if I appear to have reached my rock climbing limit of leading at 5C* then, subject to my physical potential, I can go further if I am prepared to work at it. This work may be in a variety of ways, and is certainly going to take a great deal of effort and hard work. If I am sufficiently determined, then I will probably improve. Interestingly, even if I do not go on to lead 6A (or whatever) I will still have benefited greatly from my efforts, providing I can see that it's the quality of the effort, rather than the result, that is really important. Captain Scott may have made grave technical errors, but his efforts, and those of his team, were nothing short of heroic, and that is far more important than who was first to the South Pole.

If one can sustain the ambition of the increasingly more difficult adventure journey, then the rewards can be immense, if undefinable. A stage of extreme Frontier Adventure can be reached, which could be described as the equivalent of going beyond the sound barrier, and truly being in harmony with the great outdoors, and flowing with the environment. For this to happen seems to need many years of hard work and a great deal of commitment, as well as a deep empathy with one's surroundings. To be totally at peace within a storm, on the edge of one's life, where all your experience and abilities are being taxed to their utmost, must be one of the ultimate experiences. At such times, man may feel that he is both 'atom and God', that he is an indivisible part of the harmony of Nature; and that before and after the experience are totally irrelevant. The beauty of these moments in time are indescribable. They are available to any human being who makes sufficient effort.

*Footnote: Rock climbing grades range in ascending order of difficulty from 1 to 7 with subdivisions of A, B and C. The hardest climbs currently in Britain are in the 7A category. (1983)

CHAPTER 5

Misadventure: Stage IV

Like adventure, misadventure is a state of mind. Unlike adventure, the immediate reactions are essentially negative rather than positive. At one extreme the result is death or serious injury. At the other extreme, are feelings of relief that one has escaped any serious consequences from a situation that was unduly stressful and more demanding than one had conceived at the onset of the journey. The enjoyment, satisfaction and euphoria that can arise from adventurous experiences are replaced by negative feelings of 'Thank goodness that's over', or, 'I'll never do that again', or, 'God, I was lucky'.

In a way, misadventure expresses the uncertainty of Nature. It is always a possibility on any outdoor journey and can occur at any time, especially perhaps at unexpected moments. When it occurs, one's fears are suddenly intensified and flood to the surface, even if only fleetingly. On a rock climb, for example, an unexpected hold breaking off, or a crucial running belay detaching itself, can transform a stage I, II, or III situation, where enjoyment or satisfaction are high and everything is under control, into a situation where, at very least, the feelings are highly unpleasant and to be removed as soon as possible.

Obviously such situations, if they become frequent, or are particularly extreme, will tend to result in the performer giving up that style of journey. His confidence becomes severely impaired and his reactions so negative, that he sees no point in continuing with those type of experiences.

To a degree, however, the misadventure experience can be a most valuable teacher. The reality of what happens can make an indelible mark on the mind of the performer. It can prompt honesty and open-mindedness. It can break down a rigidity of thinking and alter attitudes, especially when the experience is constructively reviewed. Nature teaches in a much more powerful way than a human teacher, and should be used where appropriate. A good example might be the teaching of the danger of trees in fast currents on rivers, to canoeists.

It is not easy to make the canoeist really aware of this danger, which can occur on the easiest of rivers, because the situations tend to look harmless. Whilst he can quickly pick up the necessary skills to avoid the danger, he is unlikely to be aware of the urgency in the situation should a mishap occur. One successful method I have found was to insist that the performer deliberately capsized against a tree in a current. I had chosen a tree and river which I knew I could handle from a bank position. Unsurprisingly, the group concerned did not enjoy the experience, but they were under no illusions about the dangers involved, and as a result would become safer teachers.

The group concerned were learning to become teachers of a particular style of adventurous journey and therefore had high motivation. From that standpoint, using a stage IV deliberately was justified. The same situation with a group of beginners would probably have had such a traumatic psychological effect, that it would have put them off canoeing as a form of journey, and would have been quite unjustified.

There are times, however, when stage IV can, and should, be used with great discretion, even with beginners. I remember a large lad on a Centre Course who was disliked by most of his peers because he tended to be both arrogant and a bully. The group were traversing a steep slab with strict instructions not to go more than six feet above the beach. (They were all moving unroped). He decided to ignore the instructions, and soon was ten feet up and stuck. He declared he could not move up, or down, or sideways. Eventually, in a state of panic, he fell off, and I fielded him at the bottom. His ego was severely bruised. For the rest of the Course, he followed all instructions carefully as he was not keen on encountering another of the laws of Nature!

Beyond the necessary safety conditions that are an essential part of both education and work with beginners of any age, there is a fascinating paradox. In the world of the advanced adult performer, stage IV can have great rewards. I am not recommending that extreme misadventure be sought out, as there is no doubt that it tends to be both very frightening and fraught with dire consequences. It can however, act as a trigger to maximum performance and effort which in itself is either exhilarating or felt to be very worthwhile – at least in retrospect. In a way this type of stage IV has the effect of heightening the awareness to acute levels, with corresponding increased performance, providing it is not beyond the breaking point of the control of the performer. This breaking point may be much further away than one thought. It seems to depend both on the inner strength of the individual and what is at stake.

From personal experience I remember two particular incidents vividly, although they were many years ago. One was on the River Usk in South Wales. Several more experienced friends had urged me to join them on a winter trip with a 10 foot flood on the river. I went reluctantly, as I was frightened about the dangers, yet I didn't want to appear to be a coward. As expected, the river was going like a train, and I started behind everyone else, in a highly tense state, which meant my performance was tense. The first obstacle – a long fall into a large stopper – had me so gripped that I capsized at the top. As I went over, I was in severe stage IV. To come out of my boat at this level of water made survival a question of Russian roulette, rather than skill. I managed to eskimo roll, and from that point on I was sufficiently relaxed to kayak efficiently through the more difficult sections. Stage IV became extreme stage III, and it became a tremendous experience.

The other incident concerned the first British ascent of the North face of the Dent d'Herens *(voie Welzenbach)* with Wilfred Noyce and Jack Sadler, an American.[1] At the top of the initial ice slope. As we were unroped, and the 400 foot slope disappeared into a large bergschrund, I had big problems, especially as I was almost totally unskilled in the art of ice axe braking! Motivation was of the highest order, however, and I eventually stopped and then rejoined the others. What was interesting, on reflection, was that for the rest of that long day, and despite some very difficult and dangerous sections, I was sufficiently relaxed both to perform efficiently and to lead. Once again stage IV had led to a significant reduction in my personal tension.

In both instances, however, my survival instinct was of the utmost importance to me. I didn't want to die, or to hurt myself. Much more experience, over twenty years, in the outdoors, and especially of solo journeys has changed my attitude to death. I would agree with the German philosopher, Schopenhauer who said that, 'The most important thing in life is to die at the right time'. If one dies doing a journey in the environment that one loves, and has given every ounce of one's efforts, then that is one of the right times to depart, and one may approach it in peace, rather than terror. At this extreme, death may be felt, not as the greatest of misadventures, and therefore a totally negative experience, but as the opposite. Robert Service, described death as the last great adventure.[2] Frank Smythe described it as 'not to be feared' and 'the supreme experience' and 'climax of life'.[3] Both men were deeply experienced in outdoor living. I have also spoken to several people, who have thought they were dying on wilderness journeys – in very large surf; falling off big mountains; and in one case, washed off a sea cliff. Their reactions went from initial intense fear to 'a feeling of peace', and 'like a white light after the blackness.'

These people survived to describe their reactions. Captain Scott's party didn't, but perhaps its tragedy was more apparent than real. When the rescue party found the bodies, the face of Dr. Wilson expressed peace and contentment. If one accepts that it is effort that counts, and that happiness comes from doing what one loves, then death in itself need not be viewed as the ultimate horror, at least for the mature person. The spirit of the human being has long been recognised as being stronger than the body, and who is to say what happens to the spirit?

Alongside the magnificence of spirit of Scott and his team, I would like to end with thoughts on another Polar explorer – Sir Ernest Shackleton. In one sense his epic journey, from the crushing of his ship in the Antarctic ice, to the escape by open boat to South Georgia was a desperate misadventure. It may have broken his spirit. Before he walked across South Georgia, he said 'I will never take another expedition',[4] a clear statement, perhaps, that he had gone beyond what he could psychologically take. It was not many years later that he died as a comparatively young man, probably in part the result of all the stress he had been through. Yet there can be no doubt that his spirit was magnificent. Few explorers have displayed such superb commitment and in such an outstanding manner, to the safety of all those in their care. He literally spent years ensuring the safety of all those he left behind on Elephant Island. When the job was done, perhaps that was the right time to depart.

The paradox of stage IV is clearly seen in some of the great writings. Confucious remarked, 'A man who understands the Gods of Nature in the morning, may die without regret in the evening'. The great statesman, Dag Hammerskjold said, 'Do not seek death. Death will find you. But seek the road which makes death a fulfilment'.[5] And the final word from one of the giants of the outdoors, John Muir, 'The rugged old Norseman spoke of death as HEIMGANG – home-going. So the snow-flowers go home when they melt and flow to the sea, and the rock ferns, after unrolling their fronds to the light and beautifying the rocks, roll them up close again in the autumn and blend with the soil'.[6]

CHAPTER 6

The Instinct for Adventure

'When I was young my friends weren't bored or idle or particularly poor; but we still took it out on the rolling stock of the Midland railway'. [1]

Thirty years of involvement with adventure in the outdoors has convinced me, that not only is there an instinct for adventure in the human race, but that failure to provide suitable outlets for this instinct in the younger generation, has made a marked contribution to the sickness of western living.

As a young man I had perhaps the typical view that some boys, and a much smaller number of girls, are naturally adventurous. If anyone at that time had told me that all young people had a yearning for excitement, risk and challenge, I would have dismissed it as poppycock. There seemed countless examples, from my own schooldays, of young boys who appeared to want nothing to do with adventure of any kind.

Running an L.E.A. Outdoor Centre for six years for one English city (Oxford), forced me to accept that it was likely to be an instinct. All the secondary schools from the city – a considerable cross-section of boys and girls, from all manner of backgrounds, and with a wide variety of intelligence, physical abilities and otherwise – used the standard fortnight Courses at the Centre, throughout the year. Many, perhaps the majority, came not because they liked adventure activities (of which they generally had no experience, except for camping), but in order to have a bit of fun away from school and 'normal' living. Many of them, both in appearance and ability, would never be described as likely adventurers. In particular, perhaps, there were the overweight boys and girls, who trembled even at the thought of rock climbing or caving.

In the first year of the Centre, the standard programme was to offer a first week of introductions to as wide a variety of adventure activities as the local environment allowed – camping, hill walking, river canoeing, caving, rock climbing, an assault Course, and Field Studies. For the second week pupils opted for any one of these activities (except the assault course), which was then pursued, culminating normally in a three day expedition away from the Centre.

Generally this second week was very successful, as most youngsters were both learning skills and taking on challenges in the activity they had particularly enjoyed doing. There was always one group, however, who seemed to be less adventurous and opted for Field Studies. The latter were provided because there was Authority pressure not to do just adventure activities. In talking to the youngsters, and through questionnaires it became obvious that, generally, Field Studies was unpopular, and that this particular group also wanted to do something 'adventurous'. What happened in practice was that, in the evenings, the Field Studies group tended to find themselves listening to the no-doubt exaggerated stories of the youngsters who had been involved in a range of 'high' adventure. As a result, they felt, by the end of the Course, that they were really missing out. For most of these youngsters, Field Studies could not compare in terms of excitement.

Eventually, because I was concerned that we provided high consumer satisfaction within the adventure ethos of the Centre, we dropped Field Studies.[2] In its place came a 'General Adventure' group. The activities within this group were extremely varied but, hopefully, all adventurous, with simplicity of equipment and a low emphasis on skills. Coastal traversing became very popular, which might include swimming, jumping off sand dunes, traversing low lying cliffs above water. Inland dinghying down rapids in spate in winter proved equally popular. Above all, perhaps, gorge walking became a favourite. Indeed, to such an extent that it became a standard activity for all Course pupils. In those days it was an unusual Centre activity, and because it was unconventional it attracted much criticism of 'messing about', by the more conventional Centres. It is pleasing to see that it is now a standard, and accepted, activity in Wales, the Lakes and elsewhere.[3]

In many ways it is the epitome of the adventurous journey, as expected by the younger generation. Having now taken whole classes of junior schoolchildren on gorge walks – in winter and poor weather, as well as summer – it is an obvious way to see the instinct for adventure surfacing in the whole class. A good gorge is not only atmospheric in its environment, with no views of other human existence or of paths, but it can provide a whole range of basic skills challenges at varying levels of difficulty sufficient to suit everyone. Balancing, jumping, swinging, swimming, route finding, crawling, sliding can all be involved. Everyone can have fun and excitement, and the whole group, with staff, can work together and finish soaking wet or covered in mud. Discomfort and fear can be overcome by feelings of enjoyment and satisfaction.

In an attempt to monitor the work of the Woodlands Centre, questionnaires were completed over a period of two years by all Course pupils. This involved about 600 adolescent boys and girls from all the secondary schools within the city. Every attempt was made to try and ensure honest answers. Each pupil, for example, completed the form alone, and they did not have to put their name on them. The collated results were of considerable interest to the staff. As expected, activities such as gorge walking generally proved far more popular than hill walking. 94% expressed a desire to return to another course in the summer, and this figure dropped to 71% for a further winter course. In reply to the question, 'Have you had to think carefully and frequently during the fortnight?', 92% felt this to be the case. It would seem that mental effort was a marked feature of this Adventure Course. The link between two other questions was also interesting. Replies to, 'What was your most enjoyable moment?', and 'What was your most frightening moment?' had a high correlation. In many instances the same experience provided both the most fear and the most enjoyment and satisfaction. This particular result was a key element in the development of the concept of the stages of adventure. As far as an instinct for adventure is concerned, this was perhaps contained in the question, 'Would you like to continue any of the Outdoor Pursuits when you return to Oxford?' A massive 96% of those 600 young people said 'YES'. No scientific proof certainly, but it tended to strongly support what we, the staff, felt.

The presence, or otherwise, of this adventure impulse can also be seen in urban equivalents of the gorge walk. Apart from the development of adventure playgrounds, the free choice of adolescents at school in a Physical Education period, can be most revealing. With a number of secondary and junior school classes, as a PE teacher, I would give the youngsters free choice of activity, for the final part of the lesson. Despite a wide variety of possibilities within the schools concerned, there was one favourite that never ceased to be the most popular. This was 'Pirates'. All the equipment in the gymnasium was used (or misused) to construct a journey, or journeys, with a degree of uncertainty. Again, climbing, traversing, jumping, hanging, and particularly swinging, were all involved. A good swing from one object to another is the essence of an exciting challenge – complete commitment with a degree of uncertainty.

Later in life, I remember watching my youngest daughter, aged two, display the same instinct in a fascinating way. She had just become interested in building bricks. If I built the bricks much higher than herself, then she ran away to seek the security of her mother. She was frightened that the bricks would fall down and crash as they hit the floor. At first I was amazed, until I realised that if I was her, then the brick tower might look formidable. What was interesting, was that although she ran away, she couldn't hide her instinct for excitement. She would peep round the door to watch the building. Eventually she built her own tall towers, and would then knock them down with obvious excitement, but still with a trace of fear. I would have said that during this process, she went through all the stages of adventure but in order of IV, II, III, II, I.

Whilst it may not be difficult to pursuade the reader of the existence of this adventure urge in young people, it may be much harder to convince them that it also, therefore, exists in the adult population. For a start, the number of adults that actually engage in high risk activities, despite being on the increase, is very much a minority. The number of people involved, can be increased by including activities of low risk, like walking and back-packing, which involve a journey in the outdoors with a degree of uncertainty. This is totally acceptable as adventure is a state of mind, and whilst serious accidents may seem unlikely, nevertheless the essential ingredient of fear or apprehension as to whether the challenge can be overcome, can still be present. Indeed, in the more demanding types of back-packing and similar activities, the degree of discomfort and hardship can be seen as equivalent, in some way or other, to short sharp attacks of fear common in the high risk activities. John Hillaby, for example, must express the experience of many solo walkers in his description of traversing the wilder peaks and glens of Western Scotland, and the inevitable adventures.[4] Similarly the grandmother, Mrs. M. Carter, writing in the 'Great Outdoors' of her 100 mile walk, reflects typically both on the foot suffering involved and the fears of whether she can complete the journey.[5]

The case for an adult adventure drive can be strengthened by further circumstantial evidence. With western society aiming at making both life more secure and increasingly comfortable, what better way of appealing to the lazy side of man than by offering him a wide variety of armchair adventuring. High risk, dare-devil adventure – of both socially and non-socially acceptable types, occupy a great deal of television time. Films too, or at least many of the big box office variety, are of the same type – outer space productions, sharks and Bond films spring to mind. Lectures on key modern adventure epics also attract large audiences of the man in the street. All such examples, from Kojak and Grand Prix motor racing to the climbing of Everest and racing across oceans, have a common base of excitement and challenge.

Big business in America, and more recently in Britain, has realized that it too can cash in on the adventure instinct. The great American Theme Parks started in 1955, and amongst their attractions are thrill rides. In one of these parks is a roller coaster which contains a 75 foot loop the loops, with 'the longest corkscrew and biggest loop in the world'. In another park, in Florida, there is a high wire which people can have a go at, on safety ropes. In a third park, the theme is water and includes an artificial Grand Canyon, with dinghy rides complete with big rapids.[6] It has been calculated that 70 million Americans a year pay to have a go on one of these big thrill rides![7]

In Britain, the same trend is being followed. John Broome has spent £8 million developing the Alton Towers complex in Staffordshire, to inlude Britain's first double corkscrew roller coaster and the world's biggest log flume. Attendances have grown fivefold in 18 months and he hoped for at least two million visitors in 1982.[8]

One might be tempted to note in passing, that aims of money making typically debase an experience.[9] This type of activity is certainly adventure, but artificial, as the performers take no responsibility for their actions. The experience is virtually totally safe, and reduces adventure to a 'cheap' thrill. Much more respect is deserved for those like backpackers, who seek adventure of a much less immediately exciting nature but at least in the natural environment. It is again important circumstantial evidence to note that a study by the Countryside Commission revealed that two thirds of the British population took their annual holiday in outdoor environments.

There would also appear to be an important link between

adventurous impulses and the large and increasing scale of anti-social adventure – delinquency, vandalism, crime, and flouting the traditions and rules of Authority generally. Much of this behaviour, whether by adults or young people, must be in part at least, because of the need in people's lives for excitement and challenge. Not all people are satisfied with the vicarious adventure provided by T.V. and films. Having been chased by a policeman in my youth, I can still remember the surge of adrenalin and the feeling of success, when I managed to escape! Many criminal and anti-social acts have an obvious challenge and can both involve fear and excitement. With all her experience at the National Children's Bureau, Dr. Kellmer Pringle observed the fundamental need for 'new experiences',

'The more uneventful and dull life is, the more we become bored, frustrated and restless. This is ·shown clearly by the contrast between the eagerness, alertness and vitality of normal babies whose life is filled with new experiences and challenges; and the aimlessness and boredom of the adolescent with nothing to do and nowhere to go. In seeking – legitimately – for the excitement of new experiences, where few are to be found or attainable, the forbidden, risky or dangerous are liable to acquire an aura of daring and excitement. What may start as a lark – an expression of high spirits and the desire for adventure – can turn into vandalism and violence. This happens all the more readily, the longer and the more pervasive the boredom and frustration of their lives.'[10]

Research by Dr. Sol Rosenthal in America has also indicated the likelihood of a common emotional base for the human need for excitement and challenge expressing itself in anti-social as well as socially acceptable forms. In two studies he compared the physical and mental reaction of 700 individuals engaged in wilderness challenge activities to 600 university students who had been involved in demonstrations and rioting. The degree of well-being and euphoria in each group as a result of their experiences was found to be similar, with the differences insignificant.[11] The tragedy is that societies such as America and Britain are suffering increasingly because they provide neither adequately challenging and inspiring systems of education nor sufficiently suitable outlets for adventure – such as outdoor sports.

As usual, Nature can help provide the answer as to whether there is an instinct for adventure in the human race. Jacques Cousteau made the following observation, 'The more time I spend observing Nature, the more I believe that man's motivation for exploration is but the sophistication of a universal instinctive drive deeply engrained in all living creatures.[12]

I would totally agree with him. Urban man may regard climbing, canoeing and the like as extravagant and ridiculous activities, and certainly unjustifiable as a part of education. In reality these activities – done in a self reliant manner at challenging levels – are both completely natural and essential to the future of society. (The international development and popularity of the Duke of Edinburgh Award Scheme and the Outward Bound movement with their emphasis in practice of such 'expeditions', illustrate the point.)

All living things perhaps, gain their independence by testing their ability to be self-reliant. Most species have to explore in order to test their effectiveness in an environment. Exploration is a quest for, or the investigation of, this new environment – usually made in order to extend the frontiers of existence. It is a journey into the unknown made by a living thing using all its resources. The more intelligent the species, the greater will be its ability to direct and evaluate the exploration.

Exploration and migration are instinctive aids to survival shared by all living things, even the plants. Migration literally means to journey from one place to another. Many fish and birds have a natural impulse to do this with the change in seasons, as a means of survival. Man also may migrate – taking up a new way of life in another part of the planet or in a nomadic sense, where the seasonal journeys of such tribes are even more akin to those of other migratory animals.

What is important to realize is that the migration of a living thing does not only involve a journey by definition, albeit an enforced one, but that the journey will include dangers and challenges. The dangers to birds, fishes and animals are totally real, and many die because they cannot cope. Dr. Baker, in his fascinating analysis of 'The Mystery of Migration' says

'Migration takes time, uses energy, and is dangerous. Before migrating all animals whether consciously or instinctively weigh up costs against the benefits, and, on that basis, decide on which route to take and when to leave![13]

In essence then the human race does have an instinct or impulse for adventure and exploration. There is an inbuilt drive to journey with a degree of uncertainty. The problem of Western man is to reduce the anti-social journeys and challenges in which he can opt out of his proper responsibilities. This can best be done by making the self reliant adventure journey in the outdoors a fundamental part of the education of all young people. Radical proposals of this kind are essential if education in the secondary schools is to make any real contribution towards solving the problems of the world, and make the world a better place to live in. A healthy society, if it is to progress, must have people, including the younger generation, working on all frontiers that offer possible positive outcomes.

CHAPTER 7

Towards the Development of a Philosophy

'So why do we do it?
What good is it?
Does it teach you anything?
Like Determination? Invention? Improvisation?
Foresight? Hindsight?
Love?
Art? Music? Religion?
Strength or Patience or Accuracy or Quickness or Tolerance.
Which wood will burn and how long
Is a day, and how far is a mile,
And how delicious is water and smoky
Green pea soup?
And how to rely
On your
Self?'[1]

There is a school of thought that says that the experience is sufficient in itself, and that attempts to analyse such experiences are both unproductive and unnecessary. In one sense this view has my sympathy. If I experience stage III, then I experience satisfying reactions, which are along the road to happiness. Once I try to understand the values of the outdoor experience then I am likely to become confused. It is far easier to ignore such problems, and to concentrate my energies on doing my job efficiently and planning and preparing for my next expedition.

Inevitably I suppose, my concern for the need for everyone to develop a personal philosophy, which is concerned with the meaning and values of living beyond those of materialism and ego-centred trivia, has stemmed mostly from working within education. In particular the responsibilities of running Outward Bound style Courses, and similar experiences for young people, for many years, forced me to realize that I had to have some fundamental justifications, if I ever had to face up to death or serious injury. Whether it was facing a coroner or parent, or both, I had to be able to justify to myself the reasons for placing young people in situations where a nasty accident might occur.

As the years have progressed, whilst carrying on practically with both personal adventure, and teaching both young people and mature students, I have also been concerned as a parent of three children. As they go into the modern world, it seems to me essential, that they should have some basic framework of values, in order to be able to judge for themselves, not only what is right and wrong, but more importantly, what courses of action they should take in moments of decision. Fortunately during these years, I have been asked to give keynote lectures, both in the U.K. and abroad, and this has allowed me to focus in detail on the values of Western Society and its education system.

In particular I have become increasingly alarmed at the materialistic selfishness, and the instant pleasure attitude of the West, and its leaders. In practice they give the strongest of impressions that money and power are the only really important values, and that success is to be measured by results in these fields. This in turn has led to the continuation of a traditional type of education which is extremely unbalanced in terms of the overall growth of young people. The physical and emotional needs and abilities of youth tend to be regarded as of peripheral rather than central importance, subjugated to a great extent by the need for success in examinations. In addition, the system also fails to emphasize in practice the universal values basic to any society.

The problems seem so bad, and becoming worse, that I believe that all those who are involved in adventurous journeys – whether in education or for personal reasons – should try to redress the balance, by communicating something of the basic values that can be gained from the challenging wilderness experience. All individuals have a right to freedom, but at the same time they have a responsibility as members of society. It is ethically wrong to just go out and adventure, without communicating something of the values involved in some way or other. Analysis and communication of these experiences – beyond that of the technical achievement – will paradoxically both broaden and increase the maturity of the person concerned. The future of the world depends upon people working together and communicating at all levels. The world is in such a bad state at present, that anything of potentially high value, should be passed on. It should not be forgotten that because man is part of Nature, then Nature probably has the answers to his problems.

The word 'Philosophy' often leads to negative reactions, and I must admit I find much of modern philosophy unintelligible. I view the word as an attitude to life, which is expressed by the actions of the person concerned. In other words, I think why I am doing something, and am prepared to defend that action. My own values have developed along the following lines essentially from practical experience – extending myself as well as others of all ages, and being part of a family with the obvious responsibilities. I have also tried to read widely, in order to see what some of the giants of the human stage have, in the way of advice, to offer modern man. It has been exciting to find the development, in my thoughts, of a general set of values, which could be relevant to a better type of world than the one in which we, at present, live.

Guidelines in my search for a personal philosophy have included:–

– Whichever road in life is taken, the search is for something variously called WISDOM, TRUTH, BEAUTY, HAPPINESS and FREEDOM; and that somehow these goals are in some way related, perhaps to the point of being the same thing.

– That even if the existence of some supreme God is accepted (and who else could produce the beauty in this natural world?) nevertheless each person is, or should be, responsible for all his actions both as an individual and as a member of society.

– That the potential of the human being is vast and probably beyond our comprehension. Whatever life is about, it includes maximum effort towards full development of all the socially acceptable aspects of each individual. ('Mature' is conveniently defined as 'with fully developed powers of body and mind[2]; normal self aspiring to 'ideal self'.)

– That life should be lived to the fullest for each moment of its being.

– That there are a set of positive human qualities, or traits, which are, or should be, accepted universally as a framework for all human actions.

– That all actions should be based inside a framework of trying to develop AN AWARENESS, RESPECT, AND LOVE OF SELF balanced against
AN AWARENESS, RESPECT AND LOVE FOR OTHERS balanced against
AN AWARENESS, RESPECT AND LOVE FOR THE ENVIRONMENT.

– That the problems of life, which arise through such a lifestyle,

are to be viewed in a positive and optimistic, rather than a
negative and pessimistic, manner.
– That the most important journey ultimately is the journey
inwards.

CHAPTER 8

To Develop an Awareness of, Respect and Love for Self

It has been said with great insight: 'Know thyself and know the world'.[1] Despite great strides in research into the human being, no one yet really appears to understand exactly how he functions and, as a layman, I approach the subject with considerable humility. Although one cannot in practice divide the human being into different aspects, because everything within him is interlinked, it is helpful in attempting to understand self, to see his principal sides.

Although each human being is a unique person, there appear to be four basic aspects, common to the entire race. These are:

THE PHYSICAL: we all have a body capable of physical actions (often termed the psychomotor aspect)

THE MENTAL: we have a brain to think; to rationalize feelings, and to direct and control physical actions (often called the cognitive aspect.).

THE EMOTIONAL: the affective area, concerned with feelings and instincts, and the development of personality, character and traits.

THE INNER SELF: the 'vital core'; the centre of the human being variously known as Conscience, Soul, Heart or Spirit. That part of the individual that is concerned with thoughts on fundamental values, and right and wrong. It may be seen as the source or generator of the emotions and is, therefore, very closely linked to them.

The human being can then be represented in diagrammatic form (fig. 1)

Like all life on the planet, we grow, develop or mature as a result of the experiences we have during our existence. In other words, like the acorn seed, we have the potential in each of us, to grow into a giant oak tree. How we actually grow will depend on the type and; above all, on the quality, of those experiences in life. It will also

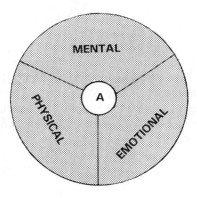

Figure 1.
THE HUMAN BEING   A - INNER MAN

(The relationship in the size of the physical, emotional, mental, and inner man aspects is unknown. The lines on the diagram are completely artificial, and may well vary in importance with each individual)

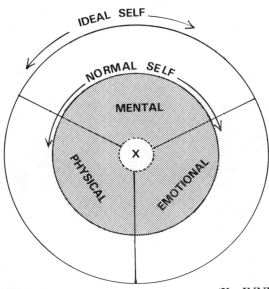

Figure 2.
THE HUMAN BEING   (X - INNER MAN)

obviously ultimately depend on our inherited or innate characteristics. Almost whatever the latter, however, we all have tremendous growth potential, in all our aspects despite perhaps a general view in western society that our individual horizons are very limited. The positive process of growth has been described as 'normal self' aspiring to 'ideal self'. It is common, especially in the young perhaps, to dream of what they could do, and what they could be, 'if only'. This process can again be represented diagrammatically in simple form (Fig. 2)

As we grow through positive experiences, then we expand our being, and become more mature. Providing we have a conducive environment, then, throughout life, we can continue to develop.

Two factors seem crucial to maximum growth. One is that as many as possible of the experiences should be magnificently demanding – in other words, deeply satisfying, experiences, which inevitably mean they make large demands on oneself in some way or other. These might well be termed stage III or frontier experiences. The other factor is that, as we are part of Nature, then we should reflect Nature in our actions and experiences as far as possible. Nature, according to scientists such as Bronowski, is about balance, and uncertainty. The latter will tend to be present in 'deep experiences'. The former, balance, is a matter of the human being seeking, or being provided with if he is being formally educated, experiences that make balanced demands on his four major aspects – the physical, mental, emotional and inner self.

Viewed in this way, it immediately becomes apparent, for example, why secondary education is so totally unbalanced. Secondary experience emphasizes predominantly one type of thinking, largely ignores the physical, and all but completely ignores the inner self and the emotions. Headmasters might refute this statement by pointing out that Religious and Physical Education, and 'The study of Man' are all in the timetable. This is irrelevant, unless the young person is having deeply satisfying experiences in these curriculum areas – which is mostly not the case.

In contrast to the school experiences, the adventure peak experience in the wilderness, tends to have considerable balance. To such a degree indeed, that it should be made available to all young people as part of their growing up. This is what would appear to be happening:

As the challenge becomes difficult and demanding, then the performer feels fear, apprehension, or discomfort. These unpleasant feelings are EMOTIONS; and if the challenge really is demanding, then fear, one of the deepest of emotions, is present. The MENTAL Aspect then comes into the picture in two ways. First, the brain attempts to push back down the fear that is trying to well up and make one panic. The brain knows that if fear is allowed to take control, then the result will be panic, and at best, poor performance. At the same time as doing this difficult job of rationalizing a very powerful emotion, it is also trying to work out how to solve the problem. 'Where are the next hand or footholds?' in a climbing situation, for example, and 'How do I use them?' This may be complex work, for there may only be one combination of moves which will lead to not falling off. One has also to think very carefully as to whether one has sufficient skill and fitness to make the moves, once they have been worked out. When the decision is taken to move, then the ideas, the use of the brain, has to be translated into PHYSICAL action.

Providing this is adventure and not misadventure, providing the top is reached through skill and craftsmanship rather than just luck, then once again the EMOTIONS become deeply involved. Feelings of exhilaration, joy, even euphoria, are, like fear, very powerful emotions.

Incredibly this whole experience may sometimes be of only a small amount of chronological time. Its value transcends time. Three basic sides – the physical, emotional and mental, are all deeply involved and balanced. The depth of involvement will obviously depend upon the size and nature of the challenge.[2] The balance of the experience is superb. The initial feeling of fear has to be counterbalanced proportionately by mental control. The ideas on how to solve the problem have to be balanced by appropriate physical action. The intensity of fear initially, is counterbalanced by the intensity of exhilaration after the event.

In some way or other, the fourth aspect – the inner self – is also involved, even if this is sub-consciously in the early experiences of this type. A sense of awe or wonder strikes at the centre of the human being – inmost reactions that have, perhaps, an almost mystical quality, and certainly far removed from normal living. Feelings so intense, that those who experience them, join the ever-increasing number of humans that seek some form of wilderness experience.

Paradoxically this peak experience should really be seen, not just in the involvement of all the major aspects of the human, but as a totality. What might be described as a HOLISTIC experience, where the elemental, and non-trivial, nature of man is entirely absorbed. Peak experiences of course, may be found in many other human activities, but it is highly likely that the wilderness one is of outstanding importance, because it involves a natural journey, and man is part of Nature.

To return to the basic sides of the human being, I want to look in more detail at the Mental, Emotional and Physical aspects. The more we can understand about ourselves, the more potential we have for growth, maturation and a better world to live in.

CHAPTER 9

Mental Development

There is a tragic, traditionally held attitude that the important use of intelligence, at least for purposes of formal education, must be, almost by definition, confined to academic subjects. That, if a young person has high intelligence, then his object in life should be to obtain the highest results, and obtain a job that reflects his intellectual abilities. Conversely, and ·particularly amongst academics, there is a generally held, and very convenient view, that activities such as adventurous journeys are essentially of a physical nature, with minimal use of the intellect. This viewpoint is both misleading, and totally unacceptable. It is time that the 'ivory towers' were exposed for what they often are – narrow, self-centred, and in some respects a major stumbling block to the development of a better world.

Thought is, or should be, but an aid to action. The intellect does not work best in a vacuum. Undue emphasis on any one of the basic sides of the human will inevitably produce an 'unbalanced' person. Too much concentration on reason alone, can lead to a self centred attitude to life. As Frank Smythe remarked, 'Nothing is more retrograde than the sort of intellectual materialism which narrows a man's outlook and beliefs to mere words and prejudices.'[1] Man is much more than an intellect, as well as being an integral part of the great harmony of Nature. As Aldous Huxley contends in 'The Perennial Philosophy', 'But whatever the intentions may be, the results of action undertaken by even the most brilliant cleverness, when it is unenlightened by the divine Nature of Things, unsubordinated to the Spirit, are generally evil'[2] The aim of intelligence is not cleverness, which is a matter of mere opinion, but, in the words of A. N. Whitehead, 'Wisdom and Beauty'.[3] A wise man is someone who knows what questions he can reasonably ask, and who would accept Pascal's comment that, 'The last proceeding of reason is to recognise that there is an infinity of things which are beyond it'.

Modern experience certainly points in this direction of the limitations of the intelligence alone. In 1982 a series of TV interviews of very eminent scientists working in different disciplines, had a common base. They all accepted that life went beyond reason alone, and that each, in his own way, had deeply held religious beliefs. As the study of Nature is revealing, there is an 'uncertainty', which scientists can neither measure nor understand in any rational way.

What has tended to happen in the modern world is aptly described by Van Der Post,

'Today we overrate the rational values and behave as if thinking were a substitute for living. We have forgotten that thought, and the intuition that feeds it, only becomes whole if the deed grows out of it, as fruit grows from the pollen on a tree. So everywhere in our civilized world there tends to be a terrible cleavage between thinking and doing'[4]

This cleavage could be reduced to some extent by having more awareness of the workings of the brain itself. Modern research is showing that whatever its limitations, it is certainly an amazing and extremely complex aspect of the human being. There are more nerve cells in the brain, for example, than all the people in the world, and each cell is complex.

The left hemisphere of the brain is concerned with scientific and analytic intelligence. It analyses, verbalizes, and sorts out logical answers, and is involved with abstractions. The right side of the brain – the sensitive side – is concerned with wholeness, intuition, and imagination. Rather than analyse, it synthesizes knowledge; organises perception in patterns; relates things together; is concerned with tone, rhythm, the apprehension of beauty, sensuous awareness, visualization and imagination, creativity and spontaneity.

With reference to the balance of Nature, a complete education (or balance of experiences) would develop right and left sides equally.[5] In practice, modern man tends to be unbalanced, because of undue emphasis on the left side of the brain – on 'vertical' thinking rather than the 'lateral' thinking of the right side.

This over-emphasis on the left side results in:
- Analysis without synthesis
- abstractions without studying relationships between abstractions

– exploiting natural resources without taking proper account of the consequences for people'.[6]

'Intuition' and lateral thinking – key functions of the right side of the brain, seem to be extremely important. This view is certainly supported by Koestler in his seminal work on the subject 'The Act of Creation'.[7] Further support is given by Cousteau who argued that,

'40 years of exploration had repeatedly proved to me that the deductive process of thinking – vertical thinking – although it is a powerful tool, rarely leads to breakthrough discoveries. On the other hand lateral thinking – the process by which the mind scans events or facts that are apparently uncorrelated to see if there is not, in reality, a hidden correlation – has often led us, and many others, to important breakthroughs'.[8]

Many of the great discoveries in the world have come about through this process, and yet we tend not to educate the right side of the brain. Einstein also recognised the importance of the right side, 'There is no logical path to these laws, only intuition resting on sympathetic understanding, can lead to them . . . The really valuable thing is intuition'.[9]

Without trying to go into detail, it would seem that stage III wilderness experience involves both left and right sides of the brain to a significant degree. This is to be expected, (but no less important for that), because it is a natural, and therefore balanced, experience. There is balance both between the two hemispheres, and between the mental and other basic human sides.

There have been attempts to define the virtues of the intellect. It is pertinent to note these, and their relevance, or otherwise, in the adventure experience:–

FORESIGHT: the ability to plan ahead and think imaginatively about possible outcomes of one's actions during a challenge, is obviously extremely relevant. With experience comes the need for foresight.

PATIENCE: anyone who has found himself up against severe problems would tend to echo Emerson's thought that of all Nature's teachings, 'patience' is the most important.

INDUSTRY: almost by definition, both stage II and stage III, experiences need a great deal of hard work. That much of the work is pleasurable is a bonus.

EXACTNESS: technical problems in stress situations often demand accuracy to a very high degree, (white-out navigation and really hard rock climbing moves, and hard rapids, spring to mind as examples).

INGENUITY: when challenges are becoming difficult, it is not unusual to have to be very ingenious (for example, a 'comfortable' bivouac after the tent is blown away; the construction of some running belays in modern climbing).

CURIOSITY: perhaps the single most important aspect of the intelligence, it is a pre-requisite for adventure. The journey with a degree of uncertainty is an acceptance by the performer that not only is he interested in what is round the corner, but that he is going to find out what is there.

As a stimulus, curiosity is much healthier than competitive feelings. The desire to know in terms of self-discovery is preferable to the desire to be superior which is implicit in competition.

If the intellectual energies of the young person are centred round his curiosity then adventure can fan this spark into a flame. A flame which can lead the person into treating the whole of life as a journey and tackling each of the problems on the way in a positive and open-minded manner.

PROBLEM SOLVING: this challenge to the brain is dependent on prior acquisition of relevant principles. Stage III experiences are about problem solving, and each type of journey has a set of principles, if both success and safe passage are to be the rewards.

CONCENTRATION: total concentration is the essence of a successful 'adventure'.

Mental development can obviously proceed apace through adventure experiences – and in a far more balanced manner than is normal in formal education. Even by the criteria of intellectual values, as indicated, adventure is clearly seen to have great potential. That potential, however, is restricted by the limitations of 'reason alone' as the mental is only one aspect of the human being.

Thinking, like the other basic sides of man, is a skill which, according to De Bono,[10] can be taught. It is not the preserve either of the middle class nor of the highly intelligent, and least of all, of the universities. It may be that the 'intellectual elite' are, in practice, ignorant, probably by design! To ignore implies not to 'not know' but to close one's mind to knowledge. Many adults will not listen to a viewpoint because they are frightened of something new or different that may be a threat to their lifestyle.

A different kind of perspective on the use of intelligence is seen in such observations as 'The outward and positive sign of intelligence is intellectual activity, whether it be scholarship, music, the arts or any other leisure time pursuits, which demand skill, craftsmanship or mental effort[11]. This interpretation on the use of intelligence is clearly demonstrated in some of the alternative approaches to education. The fourteen schools who are members of the Round Square Conference, which follows the ideals of Kurt Hahn, are a pertinent example. It is highly significant that Gordonstoun, one of the Conference members, and whose pupils have included Prince Charles, Prince Andrew and Prince Edward, is committed to the virtues of self-discipline, physical fitness, a sense of adventure, and community service. Such schools would accept that 'Knowledge is secondary to Being'.[12] It is little short of tragedy that most of the younger generation are in a secondary education system that, so often in practice ignores them except on terms of academic results.

'Sell your cleverness and buy bewilderment.

Cleverness is mere opinion, bewilderment is intuition'[13]

CHAPTER 10

Emotional Development

In some ways, to begin to understand the human emotions – the AFFECTIVE area – is if anything more difficult than understanding the mental aspect. Emotions can best perhaps be described as FEELINGS. What we feel, in every second of our lives, is entirely personal, hugely complex and yet of supreme importance. More important ultimately, than either the physical or mental aspects, and closely linked to INNER MAN and what we value in life.

As within the other human components, The BALANCE within the emotions is crucial. Unless the balance is something along the right lines then we become unbalanced. This may finally result in death by misadventure, 'whilst the *balance* of the mind was disturbed'.

Each feeling has an opposite, and to appreciate positive reactions it is probably necessary to experience the opposites (for example, the feelings before and after adventure). Life perhaps should be a succession of peaks and hollows aiming if possible, to spend more and more time up the peaks, and at our outer limits. In the deepest of senses, more than a few humans have found 'happiness' in the apparent depths of trial and tribulation.

Every experience affects, for better or worse, our ATTITUDE, which helps decide the quality of further experiences. Peak experiences are felt to be highly rewarding. To proceed to more of them, and in greater intensity, it is obviously necessary to develop all the relevant skills. The physical and technical skills are fairly evident. The emotional skills less so. Yet unless the relevant emotions and attitudes are also developed, the performer will be very limited in his quest for overcoming further challenges – in any walk of life.

To decide what are the relevant emotional skills is the first problem. Once they are known, then they can be developed by progressive training.[1] A study of the great explorers, as well as other great men, will tend to reveal some common skills, or, as they are more commonly described, TRAITS. None of them, of course, exist in isolation. The parts of the human being are all in some way deeply interlinked and counterbalanced. Nevertheless, by looking at these individual qualities it may help to increase the awareness of their particular and crucial importance in life. The following is a personal list of positive traits that enable me to evaluate the quality of what I learn and experience:

DETERMINATION
SELF DISCIPLINE
SELF-RELIANCE
VITALITY
INTEGRITY
HUMILITY
COMPASSION/UNSELFISHNESS

Each trait of course is bi-polar, in that it has an opposite trait, to which it is linked in a continuum. At any given moment in time a person must be somewhere on the continuum, for example, extreme selfishness . . . . extreme unselfishness. Experiences will either inhibit or encourage the growth of each of these, and associated qualities.

I will now look at each of these traits in more detail.

DETERMINATION
A glance at a dictionary will reveal that there are more words associated with determination than any other of the human qualities. Allied words include: WILL POWER, PERSISTENCE, PATIENCE, RESOLUTION, INDUSTRIOUSNESS, PERSEVERANCE, PURPOSEFULNESS, TENACITY, ENDEAVOUR, RESOLVE, COMMITMENT, CONCENTRATION, APPLICATION, ENDURANCE, RESOURCEFULNESS, FORTITUDE, RESILIENCE, INITIATIVE.

There is no short cut to the positive development of human potential. Effort and hard work are basic factors of any morally satisfying lifestyle. Even genius has been described as 1% inspiration and 99% perspiration. Unfortunately modern western society tends to judge people by results, rather than effort – an attitude that begins in schools with the quest for examination 'success'.

In a positive sense, determination, may be seen as, 'an unbroken committed drive towards a specific result. It is normally consistent with a strong and clear natural tendency, so that anything irrelevant to the chosen purpose, is disregarded'.[2] This approach, or attitude, towards challenge is crucial if a person is to find deep satisfaction. A small-minded person weighs what can hinder him, and because of anxiety, does not make a start. The 'average' person will be put off from what he has started by emerging difficulties. The great person is the one who carries on what he has started, to the outer limits of his capabilities, but not beyond the bounds of common sense.

It is important, however, to realize that even determination has its limitations, and should be balanced against other positive human qualities. There is rarely justification for the degree of determination that goes beyond rationality. In essence, in a wilderness journey, this is a sure recipe ultimately for disaster. Nor can there be acceptance for the type of determination which might be termed as excessive stobbornness, or negative ruthlessness.

It would seem, in an ultimate sense, that individual determination is the greatest single survival factor. There are numerous examples from the world of exploration, and from war situations, such as the concentration camps, which show incredible survival feats by people who have sufficient determination to overcome extreme pain and hardship. Although there are limits to any human being's endurance and determination, they can only be judged by being tested. In the testing it is perhaps often found that the capability is very much greater than is imagined.

In these very extreme situations, people have found not only that they have almost unbelieveable inner strength, but that they have found great rewards. Nietzsche, for example, who suffered extreme pain and illness, wrote in 1883, 'The whole meaning of the terrible suffering to which I was exposed, lies in the fact that I was torn away from an estimate of my life task which was not only false, but a hundred times too low'.[3] From out of his suffering has come some of the most profound and valuable insights on human existence. It may be that determination, eventually to the point of suffering and great hardship, is essential to the final stages of personal maturity. After all, the great traditions of mankind have been wrought out of struggle and sacrifice. 'And in all fields of human endeavour, the greatest satisfaction lies in the struggle rather than the achievement itself, rewarding as that might be'.[4] Personal effort – DETERMINATION – not circumstance, produces the excellent person.

The ideal path to becoming a Buddha, for example, is the road of

NANGYO–DO, 'THE WAY OF HARDSHIP'. Those who take this way seek their own greatness. Those who follow the easy way, surrender themselves and reflect on their own smallness.

Wilderness people have similar views. An old Eskimo for example, reflected,

All true wisdom is only to be learned from the dwellings of men out in the great solitudes, and is only to be attained through suffering. Privation and suffering are the only things that can open the minds of men to those things which are hidden from others.'[5]

Not all suffering, however, is valuable and may not lead to positive outcomes, particularly where it is imposed from without. Situations of suffering entered into should normally be where the individual is aware both of the possible positive rewards and penalties from the overall experience. It would appear, however, that the development of the quality of determination, to the outer limits of the potential of the person, if it is inspired from within, is necessary if the deepest type of maturity is to be realised.

SELF DISCIPLINE

Although self-discipline is a key aspect of determination, it perhaps should be considered in its own right as the first human quality, from which other qualities can follow. In essence, a person learns to consider his actions in any situation, and then undertakes the decided course of action deliberately. It is so important in human development that it can be seen as the first aim of any form of education. A classic example of the use of self-control can be seen at the start of any stage III adventure. Only the performer can control his fear. Others can instruct him, 'Don't be afraid', but only he can rationalize the situation and push the fear back down.

What goes on within the mind of the active person is a lifelong battle between the negative and positive sides. 'Shall I give of my best, or shall I not bother? Shall I do what I think is right, which may be difficult, or shall I avoid the problem altogether?' A person should try to act always according to his conscience. Acting in this manner, which is often the most difficult of ways in the modern world is to display self-discipline in its truest sense. The wilderness journey is an excellent teacher in this respect.

SELF-CONFIDENCE

As with self-discipline, this quality and its development, should be one of the prime aims of the educational process. Providing it is based on self-knowledge, then it is one of the most precious gifts that a person can possess. In this sense, self-confidence will develop in proportion to the number and quality of experiences encountered. In particular the frontier, stage III, experiences are by far the most valuable. As Harrer remarks in *The White Spider*, '. . . . to possess this true confidence, it is necessary to have learned to know oneself at moments when one is standing on the very frontier of things'[6] As he himself demonstrated, both in the mountains and in exploration, the necessary experiences are something which have to be actively pursued. Confidence is not a gift which comes naturally with age. Rather it is something to be achieved by effort and hard work. Success develops confidence, and confidence develops talents. Conversely a lack of this quality is often the reason for failure, and lack of success. Without confidence, there can be no strength. In terms of high performance, it is essential, but it must be based on a realistic assessment of one's capabilities. This is particularly relevant in any form of stress situation.

In a deeper, more spiritual sense, modern man tends to markedly lack self-confidence. The technological revolution and the arrogance, greed and selfishness of modern society have led to great spiritual anxieties – evidenced by the frightening amount of both 'mental' illness and drug abuse. As Schweitzer remarked,

'Behind a self-confident exterior he conceals a great inward lack of confidence. In spite of his great capacity in material matters, he is an altogether stunted being . . . .'[7]

SELF-RESPECT

With a self-confidence based on personal experience will develop the associated quality of self-respect. It is linked with the person giving of his best, and acting for what he considers to be in the best interests of self, both as an individual and as a member of society. A person with low self-esteem will collapse much more easily in a challenging situation, than one who has self-respect to a high degree. Increases in this quality – through facing up to problems – will lead to higher levels of personal satisfaction, feelings of freedom and integration. Decreases will lead to increased unhappiness, anxiety, and a disorganized lifestyle.

This quality is the foundation of the dignity of man and his courage, and is an essential aspect of maturity. It tends to have little correlation with popularity in the modern world, which encourages conformity rather than integrity.

SELF-RELIANCE

To be independent – in thought and action – is crucial in the development of a mature human being. It is the hallmark, perhaps, of the person who has fully developed the qualities of both self-discipline and self-respect. As Michelangelo wrote

'. . . . whoever follows others will never go forward, and whoever does not know how to create by his own abilities, can gain no profit from the works of other men.'[8]

Its importance is clearly seen by looking at Nature. 'Nature suffers nothing to remain in her kingdoms which cannot help itself.'[9] If all other forms of life have to display self-reliance in order to survive, it would seem to indicate the need for this key quality to be characteristic of the mature human being. It would seem essential, therefore, that the wilderness journeys by the human race should not only be at stage III levels, but should also include SOLO experiences.

Such experiences are likely to be both unique and of considerable value. Frank Mulville, who has sailed the Atlantic solo, indicates something of the potential of the lone journey.

'A voyage alone, even a short one, gives an astonishing lift to the spirit. The sense of achievement, because it is self-evident is immensely satisfying. You have taken your boat from one place to another without anyone's help.

A man on the ocean alone experiences the extremes of every sensation. The rigours of the storm are more gruelling, the beauty of the ocean in its smiling moods more radiant, the joy of a safe arrival more ecstatic, the apprehension more profound.'[10]

CHAPTER 11

Vitality and Integrity

I am deeply indebted to Bertrand Russell, the greatest of the modern western philosophers, for the inclusion of vitality. He regarded it as the most important of all the human qualities, and it would seem to have much more depth than might at first be imagined. On the surface of human action, it includes spontaneity, and the crucially important attitude of ENTHUSIASM. As Emerson wisely observed in 1841, 'Nothing great was ever achieved without enthusiasm'.[1] Vauvenarges puts its value in a slightly different but no less important way, 'Man never rises to great truths without enthusiasm'.[2] Enthusiasm implies enjoyment of existence, although as far as wilderness journeys are concerned, it has to be tempered by experience. 'The world belongs to the enthusiast who keeps cool'.[3] But even in the most desperate of circumstances, vitality can exist as an unquenchable spark. In such situations it is often revealed by humour, a great asset in times of adversity. Captain Scott wrote on his second very hard sledge journey, 'My companions are undefeatable. However tiresome our day's march, or however gloomy the outlook, they always find something to jest about'.[4]

Beneath the surface of human action, the presence of vitality is even more important than the outward enthusiasm and spontaneity. Its presence is revealed by the existence of fear in a person. If there is fear, then it testifies that a struggle is going on within the person. As long as this struggle continues, constructive solutions to problems are possible. The hallmark of a deep vitality is both an open attitude to all the problems of life, and an optimistic approach to them. It is far beyond purely physical exuberance. The whole being is involved in taking on the challenge of life, in all its senses, with vitality closely linked to both determination and self-confidence.

Integrity is also intimately linked with vitality, and hardly of less importance. In a spiritual sense (the inner man) it means being true to one's best nature, being utterly honest with oneself in all the serious questions of life. At the same time it means acting in the best interests of other people. Sometimes it is far more beneficial not to speak the plain truth to someone, but at the same time not to be unnecessarily reticent. The integrity of one's own mind is perhaps the only sacred thing. 'To thine own self be true. Thou canst not then be false to any man'.[5]

In a complex and materialistic modern society, this universal and time-honoured quality is only developed with great difficulty. The ever-increasing mass of technological knowledge and the greed and selfishness of society, work against the truth. Professor Fromm went so far as to say, in 1978, that, 'Nowadays we repress the knowledge of the Truth'.[6] The state of the Third World and the lack of action is perhaps a good example. (Each day approximately 35,000 people die of hunger and about 800 million are starving). Indeed perhaps Truth is man's biggest problem, because of the trouble and inconvenience that goes with it. Untruthfulness and dishonesty are characteristic of modern society, bedevilled by a deep state of anxiety caused by the modern lifestyle. As Humphrey noted in his 1981 Brownowski lecture,

'To speak the truth amongst people who do not want to hear it, is considered almost an aggressive act – an invasion of privacy, a trespass into someone else's space. Not nice. Not done . . . when people do not want to know, they do not take kindly to the self-appointed prophet who sees it as his duty to inform them.'[7]

The complexity of society makes it easy to evade truth. The simplicity of the wilderness challenge meets truth head on. In an outdoor peak experience, man is removed from the surface living a shallow existence so characteristic of much of the modern lifestyle. Instead the basic human being – in a physical, mental and emotional sense – faces the total reality of the challenging journey. This reality is truth, and from it, man learns the value of facing up to it. The simplicity of these situations is both rewarding and stimulating. Simplicity is part of the search for truth. At the deepest human level, truth has been said, to be not only that which makes 'a man', but that it is equivalent to 'purity'. At this level the adventure road in extreme frontier situations may be one way forward. As Yanagi, a Bhuddist, noted, 'as long as life and death are seen as two opposing phases of existence, then truth cannot be grasped'.[8] The very deep satisfaction that some people have found, when in the most demanding of situations, may reflect the truth of life. The expression on the face of Scott's companion, Dr. Wilson, when they found his body may well have been because he had found truth. Over the grave of those five men in the polar ice, was written the classic phrase, 'To seek, to strive and not to yield'.

Such magnificent examples of the human spirit have inspired countless generations of young people. The adolescent seeks truth instinctively. He has a longing for the world about him, including the actions of man to show TRUTH alone. Whilst it is a crucial need of adolescence, it is also a formidable problem. The young are bombarded with almost everything, except the values of spiritual truth, and tend often to be surrounded by deceit and dishonesty in the conduct of life. Materialism and power, not truth, are seen as the Gods. It may well be that one of the reasons for the great popularity of outdoor journeys is because such experiences help them, in some way or other, in their instinctive search for truth.

This search by the young will be helped by people who are honest and sincere. They need to learn that truth in one sense is concerned with EXACTNESS and ACCURACY. Accuracy in logical matters, in dealing with facts, in aesthetic, and in physical action, are all important. Delusion, distortion and division all thrive on inaccurate, non-specific statements. The skilful deceiver uses the half truth or twisted statement rather than the outright lie. Optimism concerning the power of truth is also crucial. Truth cannot be built on scepticism. It needs self-confidence, as well as the courage of sincerity. The true self-confident action is, perhaps, one where faith in oneself and one's actions is recognised by the majority of human beings as being selfless. Untruthfulness is nearly always the result of fear that has not been answered by positive actions, Bertrand Russell, wrote,

'A certain native pride and integrity is essential to a splendid human being, and where it exists lying becomes impossible, except when it is prompted by some generous motive'.[9]

All the qualities or traits that have been mentioned: Self-confidence; Self-discipline; Determination; Vitality; and Integrity – have been essentially concerned with one objective: to develop awareness of, respect for, and love of SELF. No man is an island, however, and whilst it is essential that a person develops his individual freedom of thought and action, it is also essential that he recognises that he is part of society with all its implications. In essence this means the acceptance of another key quality:

UNSELFISHNESS or COMPASSION.

CHAPTER 12

Unselfishness and Compassion

'Human history is the sad result of each one looking out for himself'.[1]

Few men can live entirely alone as a lifestyle. Man is instinctively a social animal and needs human contact. Even the great solo explorer John Muir, who spent much of his life so happily alone in the great outdoors of the American West, a century ago, recognised the need. 'There perhaps are souls that never weary, that go always unhaltingly and glad . . . Not so, weary me. In all God's mountain mansions, I find no human sympathy, and I hunger'.[2]

The need for people to be together, all seeking personal happiness in their individual ways, is probably the central problem facing the human race. Schweitzer recognised the problem, 'That everyone shall exert himself . . . to practice true humanity towards his fellow-man, on that depends the future of mankind.'[3] Selfishness, obviously, is a major cause of world as well as individual problems. Modern society, through its lifestyle, encourages selfishness to a very high degree. Karen Horney captures its essence in her book *The Neurotic Personality of Our Time,*

'It must be emphasized that competitiveness, and the hostility that accompanies it, pervades all human relationships. Competitiveness is one of the predominant factors in social relationships. It pervades the relationship between men and men, between women and women, and whether the point of competition be popularity, competence, attractiveness, or any other social value,it greatly impairs the possibilities of reliable friendship. It also, as already indicated, disturbs the relations between men and women, not only in the choice of the partner, but in the entire struggle with him for superiority. It pervades school life. And perhaps most important of all, it pervades the family situation, so that as a rule the child is inoculated with their germ from the very beginning'.[4]

In one sense of course, competition can make people work very hard and give of their best, which in itself is admirable. Where this success leads to friction and discord with others, however, then it is likely to be counter productive. It seems crucially important to develop an attitude of competition WITHIN ONESELF. In other words to try and develop one's potential (in all senses) through the higher and more positive side of one's nature, winning as often as possible, over one's lower, more basic and selfish side. If it is recognised that each person is unique, then any form of competition against another person, ultimately has no functional significance. In a world in which nuclear war threatens, it is obviously essential that each person in the world attempts to become part of a united human race. It is only the fear and selfishness of the great superpowers, that is preventing the development of unselfishness to the point where all human beings are fed, housed and clothed to an acceptable standard. The world spends the sum necessary to do this job, every fortnight approximately, on arms!

It would be wrong however, to simply criticise the super-powers and the leaders of modern society. Each human being has a responsibility, if he has integrity. It is extremely difficult not to be selfish, as it is almost impossible to be completely unselfish. One can only enormously admire people of the calibre of Mother Theresa, and those who give their lives to help others. Nevertheless the opportunities to be unselfish are always available, and should be sought out and taken up whenever possible. In any corner of our modern society, help is required in a myriad of forms.

Up to taking the post of Warden of the Woodlands Centre in 1965 my life had been predominantly selfish. As a teacher I had tried to do the best job I could, and had involved young people in expeditions and extra-curricular outdoor activities. Nevertheless, as each year passed by, it was obvious, if I was honest with myself, that most of my considerable free time was spent climbing or canoeing. It was what I wanted to do, when I wanted to do it. I felt no serious responsibility as a member of society apart from my job and occasional outings with school pupils.

Acceptance of the Woodlands post was an attractive proposition with only one major snag. I realised that my personal adventure would suffer both through the nature of the post and starting a new Centre, and from a large diminution in spare time. Instead of a long summer holiday, for example, the maximum I could expect was four weeks. After much thought I accepted the post, reasoning that the loss of leisure time would be balanced by working full time in an outdoor context. I was naive in failing to take into account the energy and time demands of administration!

The six years at the Centre proved to be very hard work. Trying to meet the needs and abilities of young people in a residential and adventurous environment taxed the energies of all the staff. It was normal in a week's break, for example, to spend the first two or three days recovering from the previous six weeks. In the same way, in the summer, at least the first week of the four weeks' holiday was spent in 'winding down'. But there were no regrets at taking on the Centre, apart from the strains on family life. The reactions of the young people, their smiles and laughter, and their letters; the letters from headteachers and parents; the considerable staff spirit working as a team; the feeling that we were doing something potentially very valuable for these youngsters – all these types of reactions to what we were doing, made the job infinitely rewarding and worthwhile.

Indeed, and perhaps, paradoxically, the person who acts unselfishly, benefits greatly from the process, in terms of personal development. Life ultimately is about feelings and there is tremendous satisfaction in helping others in need. To be respected and loved by others, comes in great part from acting unselfishly – by helping them. This is the basis of FRIENDSHIP as R. W. Emerson commented,

'Our chief want in life is someone who shall make us do what we can. This is the service of a friend. With him we are easily great. How he flings open the door of existence. What questions we ask of him. What an understanding we have. How few words are needed. It is the only real society. A real friendship doubles my possibilities and adds his strength to mine'.[5]

The challenging wilderness journey is potentially an outstanding way not only of developing friendship, but of emphasizing the need for people to work together. Experience can soon show both that lives may well be put further at risk by selfish and thoughtless actions, and that success will best be achieved by efficient teamwork. Despite being one of the first men to reach the top of Everest, Tenzing could note that, 'Friends are as important as achievement'. (One might have hoped he would have said 'more important'). He also remarked that, 'Selfishness only makes a man small'.[6] The joint conquest of difficulties can both develop and reinforce the strongest of friendships. A common hardship can develop a common philosophy. Nothing perhaps can match the treasure of common memories and of trials endured together. The rope on a mountain, for example, can be seen as linking people not only in terms of safety but in terms of sympathy and understanding. Smythe suggests further values,

'If it is realized how much a successful attempt to climb one of the highest hills depends on comradeship, goodwill, service . . . and all those qualities which are so necessary in any community if it is to exist happily, then the highest hills can serve to inspire men . . . and can be of great national and international value.'[7]

It is not simply the mountains, of course, but any form of hard wilderness journey. As Wilfred Noyce wrote, 'The bond of hardship is stronger than any bond'[8]

Tony Hiebeler in his book on the Eiger hints at something beyond friendship. After the fourth bivouac, he wrote, 'For all the unearthly strangeness of the North Face, our complete unity as a team put new heart into me. This singleness of purpose could no longer be described in terms of friendship or community. It was something more . . . .'[9]

I wonder from his comment, whether this is an example of what can be achieved in extreme frontier situations. Like him, I cannot find words adequate to describe such feelings. Somehow everything can become one unity, one harmony, larger than life and beyond description. What Koestler called living on the ABSOLUTE rather than the TRIVIAL plane of life.[10] Where the sum of the people involved is more than the simple addition of their personalities, in the same way that a single person is more than the sum of all his parts. Whatever happens in these situations, it would seem that for those involved, a giant step is taken along the road to happiness and freedom, truth and wisdom.

Not all expeditions, of course, result in the development and experiencing of such positive human qualities as unselfishness. Many expeditions, including ones that appear to be successful in achieving their goal, are disastrous in terms of developing human relationships. The international Everest expedition was a prime example, but by no means unique. There appears to be certain qualities required, if people are to work successfully in stress situations.[11]

In all forms of wilderness challenge there is no place for example for grumblers. Personality quickly becomes a real fact of life because the true nature of man is revealed. The ideal companion tends to be one who does his job quietly and patiently, and above all, keeps cheerful until he disappears into his sleeping bag at the end of the day.

These thoughts are echoed by a study done on the selection of New Zealanders for the Scott Base in the Antarctic in the 1950s and 1960s. The most suitable people were found to be QUIET, ALERT, INTELLIGENT, GOOD HUMOURED and MODER-ATE IN HABITS. It tended to mean people who were introverted and self-sufficient rather than 'aggressive psychopaths who were often unreliable and cowardly.'[12]

Resilience and toughness in a physical sense might be essential for survival, but they are not as important as the human qualities.[13] Shackleton's expedition might well have been destroyed, for example, if it had not been for some of his qualities. During the expedition he suffered greatly from the physical hardships, yet he was revered by all his men. His outstanding characteristic was 'his care of, and anxiety for the lives and well-being of his men'.[14] Display of this quality led to tremendous team spirit and a will to survive. Captain Scott's expedition developed a similar spirit, as did Nansen's three-year expedition in the Arctic wastes.

The attitude of all those involved is crucial. Spencer Chapman, highly experienced in the stress of danger situations, noted with great simplicity, 'There is nothing either good or bad but thinking makes it so. This seems to me the ideal motto for an expedition, whether it is applied to food, equipment or the discomforts.'[15]

It obviously helps in more demanding expeditions at least, if the people involved are not of the neurotic or anxious type. Professor Fromm remarked, . . . 'to be at home with oneself is the necessary condition for relating oneself to others!'[16] This would seem to be where the solo adventure experiences are an important part of the training for expeditons with other people. By being self-reliant, one learns to not only control one's fears through self-discipline, but also to judge, with some accuracy, one's capabilities. A self-reliant journey or journeys of the stage III level will lead to a considerable amount of self-awareness. A marked feature of modern society is that people tend to spend very little time away from other people. The rush of modern life leaves little time for deep personal reflection.

Expeditions often allow time for this much needed personal reflection, although the stress of the challenge can sometimes make seeing the other person's viewpoint hard to accept – especially if danger is involved and your viewpoint is radically different. Good leadership and tolerance are vital if the expedition is genuinely to work as a team. There is an interesting parallel with war situations. Because life is a paradox, there is much of value that can stem from war. One might note in passing, that in the last World War, the numbers of people with mental illness declined in Britain. The reason would seem to be that people had to work together – in other words to act with a higher degree of unselfishness than was normal, and for a common cause. An even more vivid example comes from Russell Braddon, who wrote of his years in a Japanese Prisoner of War camp. Although the prisoners were subjected to a brutal lifestyle over some years, he could still write,

'Strangely enough our life was almost totally devoid of friction. It is remarkable to record that in the Pudu community of 1,000, and the Changi community (7,000 to 17,000), and in all the camps in Thailand, over four years, there were no cases of murder, remarkably few of theft (except from the Japs.), and only three suicides . . . It was a tribute to the Anglo-Saxons' ability to live together.'[17]

A further example of the British is the 1982 Falklands war. During the war, the spirit of those involved in the fighting was mirrored by an upsurge of spirit within British society. A strong feeling of working together for a common cause in the name of justice was evident. Less evident then, but obvious now, is that the upsurge of spirit has decreased again, back to the normal pre-occupations of economic problems. Although good can come from war, in general the bad aspects vastly outweigh the good ones. The war in the Falklands, it could well be argued has not solved that problem at all. It would seen that modern man needs to find some alternative to war that leads to people working together with considerable energy and commitment.

Kurt Hahn, and many others, found one answer in trying to develop the concept of service to others, and in particular, the media-attracting concept of young people helping with rescue services. This approach is excellent, and deserves extensive development as a basic part of the education of young people. There are always people in need and the whole of society not just the young, should be involved in some way or other. There can be no moral acceptance of undue selfishness by any member of society.

In essence, the quality of unselfishness in this way becomes extended into the deeper quality of COMPASSION. Seeing someone in need, feeling sympathy for their situation, and ACTIVELY doing something to help as far as one can. There are almost daily examples in this country of extreme compassion – particularly in the rescue services where people willingly risk their lives to save others; and in hospitals, and a whole variety of emergency situations which are part of modern life.

Compassion is a universal human quality. In Bhuddism, for example, compassion is seen as one of the two types of energy that 'flow' from the heart. The other is wisdom. The fully enlightened mind of a Bhuddist will contain three characteristic elements, of which one is 'universal compassion'. Similarly, Schweitzer regarded this value of the highest importance in the development of his concept of 'Reverence for Life'[18] Compassion may be seen as 'an expression of loving giving it the strength and natural flow to caring for others and enjoying their existence'[19]

If one seeks a road to happiness, then the road of extreme unselfishness needs to be considered, for it has often been said that there is no happiness in having or in getting, but only in giving. This road may need the greatest levels of courage and determination.

A framework for the development of this quality is the growth of: AN AWARENESS OF, RESPECT FOR, AND LOVE OF, OTHERS.

CHAPTER 13

Humility and Courage

The quality of humility is, or seems to be, particularly difficult to develop in a modern society. Technological man has developed an attitude that Nature should be conquered and that it should provide all his needs. Arrogance, the opposite of humility, is a characteristic of our type of society, and is evident throughout its structure.

It is a difficult trait to describe. Dag Hammarskjold helps somewhat when he describes it as 'just as much the opposite of self-abasement, as it is of self-exhortation.'[1] It is concerned with the attitude of a person to his existence. Essentially, perhaps, it is to accept that the human race in general, and the individual in particular is part of Nature, rather than superior to it. And similarly to accept that no matter how great one's achievements are, these are not in any way to be seen as superior to those of other people.

Humility may be difficult to define, but it is not only a crucially important virtue, but a magnificent one, and essential to any form of maturity. Ruskin went so far as to say, that, 'The first test of a truly great man is his humility.'[2]

The paradox of living surfaces again, in that the more one learns about anything, the more one realises how little one really knows. As scientists pursue their quest for answers in Nature, the more they come up against the uncertainty of Nature and an area beyond logic and the most powerful of modern inventions.

Certainly the quality is likely to be both appreciated and developed by those who regularly journey in the great outdoors. Conversely, arrogance is often a characteristic of youth and not least perhaps by those who are adventurers. This may well be displayed in terms of attitudes to other people. When I look back on my youth I am appalled at how deeply engrained was my arrogance. It took a range of experiences over many years to make me realize the undesirability of such a trait. Vivid lessons remain in my memory.

One of the earliest recollections of such a lesson was in North Wales as a young climber. I was sitting on the Terrace on Tryfan feeling very pleased with myself as I had just led my first Very Severe – Belle View Bastion. Climbing in plimsolls, as recommended, I had found the climb somewhat open and exposed, but had generally enjoyed it. As we sat enjoying the view what appeared to be a middle-aged, somewhat scruffy figure arrived on the Terrace from the track at the side. Ancient rope draped round his shoulders was matched by an old pair of trousers and an even older pair of ungainly boots. He passed the time of day with us, and then, to our utter amazement, he walked to the top of Belle View Bastion, and then disappeared down the route! We later discovered that it was J. M. Edwards, who in his prime was one of Britain's finest rock climbers. His nonchalent performance put our efforts into a more realistic perspective.

In the totally different context of the sea, my feelings of humility towards the environment rather than towards master craftsmen have been underlined by various experiences. One of the most memorable of these occurred in Scotland. After the successful Nordkapp kayak expedition in 1976, I had decided to have an easy summer and to attempt the first kayak circumnavigation of the Outer Hebrides. The Norwegian experience, along with various journeys on the British West coasts led me to believe that this journey would be an enjoyable and not a particularly difficult challenge, providing that we had reasonable weather and sea conditions.

After taking the ferry from Skye to East Loch Tarbet on Harris, we had paddled down the sheltered East Coast of the Outer Hebrides, to camp on the isolated and immensely attractive island of Mingulay. The following day we were to paddle west through the Sound of Barra and round Barra Head, the southerly tip of the Outer Hebrides. As we expected this to be somewhat exposed, we double-checked tidal patterns and weather forecasts. The weather was excellent, the tides favourable, and the swell on the west side was what the locals termed 'small'.

Once through the Sound and off Barra Head we entered another world. In our kayaks the swell seemed huge, with companions disappearing for what appeared to be long periods of time. It was my introduction to the vast difference between sea swell and ocean swell. We did not linger and were soon round on the east side in the lee of the island. We landed and walked up to the lighthouse on top of the cliffs. The lighthouse keeper was surprised to see us, and emphasized how lucky we had been to have such a good day. He explained that the lighthouse was generally either in cloud or covered in spray. He then went on to explain that there was a lichen that only grew on the top of the cliffs because it was frequently doused with salt water, and that fish had been found on top of the cliffs. What was 'mind-blowing' was that the west facing cliffs on which the lighthouse was built were 620 feet above lea level! It was hard to believe. Yet, as we had just kayaked round these cliffs, we had no doubt that it was true. It just happened to be a place where the Atlantic, with a fetch of 3,000 miles, met land and the continental shelf. There were other places too on that West coast, as well as the most northerly point – the Butt of Lewis – which emphasized both the majestic power of the Atlantic, as well as the need for great caution and humility.

In looking at some of the writings on the outdoors, it is not difficult to find expressions of humility concerning the vast range of beauty within Nature. For example, John Wyatt describes a situation in a forest, 'I count those moments of watching fawn play, as some of the happiest of my life. I remember them now with a great deal of humility'[3]. Feelings for such beauty are entirely beyond the control of the mind.

In experiencing peak adventure, feelings of humility can be just as strong – possibly stronger in extreme stress situations. The literature of great journeys often reflects such feelings. Bowers noted in 1910 for example, after some early adventures '. . . . Certainly we shall start for the Pole with less of that foolish spirit of blatant boast and ridiculous self-assurance that characterised some of us on leaving Cardiff.'[4] More recently the Italian climber Walter Bonatti wrote, after attempting the Whymper Spur on the Grandes Jorasses solo, 'I gradually made my way up into the heart of the mountain wall. Everything here induced reflection, reducing the most deep-rooted illusions of strength and endurance to a realization of fragility.'[5]

The solo experience, of course, is likely to increase the awareness of humility, because of the likely heightened emotional state, as well as the very close feelings to Nature.

Wainwright, the guidebook writer, describes walks on the popular heights above Derwentwater in the Lake District,

'Alone, what a celestial beauty I found there in the quiet of late autumn and early winter! . . . . I walked on golden carpets between golden tapestries, marvelling anew at the supreme craftsmanship that has created so great a loveliness, and at my own good fortune to be in its midst, enjoying a heaven I had done nothing to deserve. One cannot find the words to describe it: only an inexpressible humility fills the heart . . . ."[6]

The sea is also highly conducive to similar feelings. Even those who journey the oceans of the world regularly in large vessels, tend to have a look in their eyes which indicates that there have been times when the sea has been so majestic, that they have felt deeply afraid. Many retire away from the sea and attend church with regularity. David McTaggart, an experienced sailor, writes of a calm sea in the South Pacific, with a description of rollers of a 100 feet in height and how 'A feeling of deep humility came over us that lingered for days after the sea returned to normal.'[7] Bernard Moittoissier, the famous round-the-world sailor, speaks of man as 'both atom and God.'[8] This is an excellent phrase. Man can achieve incredible feats in almost anything. At the same time he can experience, and should accept, that he is a speck in the great universe; a minute part of a great harmony. The author of the classic book 'Heavy Weather Sailing'[9] in his introduction on the general requirements for a competent seafarer, lists humility as the key quality. The photographs of enormous breaking seas, emphasize the point.

In a totally different environment, but also one perhaps of desperation and stress – a prison – Oscar Wilde wrote,

'I have lain in prison for nearly two years . . . I have passed through every possible mood of suffering . . . Now I find hidden away in my nature something that tells me that nothing in the whole world is meaningless, and suffering least of all. That something hidden away in my nature, like a treasure in a field, is Humility. It is the last thing left in my life, and the best: the ultimate discovery at which I have arrived: the starting point for a fresh development.'[10]

There has been one key human quality missing from those already mentioned – the universal virtue of courage. Despite its extreme importance and great popularity in society, it has deliberately been placed after those of determination, self-discipline, self-confidence, unselfishness, vitality, humility and integrity. A person who possesses the latter qualities and recognises their importance in his actions, is highly likely to display courage.

Indeed, in its finest and most noble sense – that of giving one's life to the service of others who are desperately in need of aid – courage may be seen as the ultimate form of all these fundamental qualities. Put in a slightly different way, this type of courage is the ultimate action of the positive side of the human being.

It is, however, a complex as well as composite quality – 'A diamond with many facets.'[11] In a situation of high objective danger, the degree of courage shown, for example, will depend not only on the degree of danger but on other factors too. These will include the purpose of the action. The rescue of someone unknown to the rescuer, would be a higher level of courage than the rescue of a friend and both would be at higher levels than that of a person who is fighting for his own survival. In addition to this factor is the crucial question of the awareness, intelligence and experience of the person in the situation. The greater the awareness and sensitivity of the person to the implications of the action, the higher the level of courage. This is clearly seen by the person who appears to act very courageously but whose actions are based on ignorance of the implications. Similarly the motive of the person concerned is highly relevant in terms of whether he seeks to gain something personally from the situation, or whether he totally submerges any personal ambitions.

Dag Hammarskjold made an astute comment when he wrote,
'How favoured by the Gods is he, whose character is tested in situations where courage has a meaning for him, perhaps, even a tangible reward. How little does he know about his potential weakness, how easily may he be trapped, and blinded by Self-Admiration.'[12]

There is an obvious danger that society's adulation of courageous acts can lead to increased egotism in the person concerned. This contrasts strongly with a person who acts courageously in an unpopular manner. Sometimes, on adventurous journeys, it takes more courage to turn back and retreat, when all the risks have been carefully evaluated and it is deemed foolhardy to carry on. No one likes to be called a coward and in these situations the importance of self-respect and integrity are crucial. Similarly those who are conscientious objectors in times of war need often to display a high degree of fortitude, so unpopular are their actions.

Whatever the degree of courage, the basis for all these type of actions lies perhaps in particular with the control of fears and anxieties. In other words, self-discipline and determination are esse'ntial. Lord Moran went so far as to say, 'Courage is willpower'.[13] George Patton Junior put it in a slightly different way,

'If we take the generally accepted definition of bravery as a quality which knows not fear, then I have never known a brave man. All men are frightened. The more intelligent they are, the more they are frightened. The courageous man is the man who forces himself in spite of his fear, to carry on. Discipline, pride, self respect and self confidence are attributes which will make a man courageous even when he is afraid'.[14]

There is a tendency perhaps to see courage as a very special quality reserved for times of emergency and severe stress. In one sense this is appropriate because it becomes at once the most noble and extreme of human actions, particularly if it is concerned with helping others. This tendency by society however, to place courage on a high pedestal could also be seen as a convenience to minimal disruption of order, administration and the 'status quo'. As J. F. Kennedy commented in *'Profiles of Courage'*,

'. . . In a democracy, every citizen, regardless of his interest in politics, 'holds office'; every one of us is in a position of responsibility; and, in the final analysis, the kind of government we get depends upon how we fulfil those responsibilities'. He then later goes on to broaden the use of this timeless quality, 'In whatever arena of life one may meet the challenge of courage, whatever may be the sacrifices he faces, if he follows his conscience – the loss of his friends, his fortune, his contentment, even the esteem of his fellow men – each man must decide for himself the course he will follow. The stories of past courage can define that ingredient – they can teach, they can offer hope, they can provide inspiration. But they cannot supply courage itself. FOR THIS EACH MAN MUST LOOK INTO HIS SOUL'. (my capitals)[15]

Alexander Solzhenitsyn looked into the soul of America when he gave his sombre verdict on the state of Western Society in a major speech at Harvard University in 1976. Disillusioned with Russia, he had escaped to the West and become an international celebrity with his books on the intolerable Russian way of life. After four years in the West, his comments on it made him highly unpopular – a classis case of the problems that truth can bring. In particular, apart from commenting that both Russia and the West had the same objective of human materialism, he noted that the West was characterized by a marked lack of courage, faint-heartedness and was concerned with ego-centred trivia.[16]

This lack of courage within society generally, except in times of war and other emergency situations, is largely because the lifestyle and the education system in practice ignores its fundamental importance. In a scathing attack on both, Professor Meredith of Leeds University, a psychologist, wrote the following in 1954,

'Courage and maturity are not qualities to be achieved, enjoyed and basked in without further effort; they cannot be worn like a medal. They are dynamic qualities which only endure by being kept on the move. Many homes today seem to lack all awareness of the need for such qualities. If schools likewise are so security minded, so obsessed with the paper medals of examination certificates, that children are never exposed to the demands which beget courage, their outlook is poor inded. A 'safe' career is their only protection in a civilization more dangerous than the jungle'.[17]

These are strong words but I suspect the Professor would have been even more appalled by most of the developments of the last three decades. He goes on to say that courage in both a physical and moral sense should be an essential aim of education. Bertrand Russell, also writing on the aims of education, has a similar view,

'Thus the perfection of courage is found in the man of many interests, who feels his ego to be but a small part of the world, not through despising himself, but through valueing much that is not himself . . . It is courage in this positive sense that I regard as one of the major ingredients in perfect character'.[18]

Both he and Meredith saw the value in young people learning to overcome fear. Russell remarked,

'Fear plays an extraordinary large part in the instinctive emotional life of most people . . . I believe it is possible to educate ordinary men and women that they should be able to live without fear . . . only a few heroes and saints have achieved such a life, but they have shown the way'.[19]

Similarly Professor Meredith,

'Courage comes by acting in despite of fear . . . It comes by learning to live with fear. You can learn to live with fear if your bodily resources (muscle, nerve, skill, persistence) are a fair match for the likely dangers. This assurance will only come through testing . . .'[20]

It would have been fascinating to have discussed the value of the challenging wilderness journey with both these writers, in terms of the use of courage. Humans learn best by doing. By definition, a peak adventure experience requires the overcoming of initial fears and the harnessing of one's resources, to tackle the problem. Such experiences are potentially available to all young people and if the use of courage is as important as it would appear to be, then any form of experience that consistently and progressively requires its use, should be a CENTRAL part of education. In addition to experiencing the use of courage, young people should be continuously inspired by great acts of courage. The story of mankind brings forward heroes in every age. It is not difficult to be inspired, for example, by Terry Fox. In 1980 at the age of 22 he became the most famous man in Canada. Despite finding he had cancer and losing his right leg, he set out on what he termed 'The marathon of Hope' – an attempt to run 4500 miles from Newfoundland to the Pacific coast. After 3000 miles the cancer attacked his lungs, and he had to give up. By the time he had not only raised £10 million for cancer research, but he had blazoned the value of courage across a nation.[21] There are many other examples, many of which receive minimal publicity. They all embody one thought,

'COURAGE IS A WAY OF SAYING YES TO LIFE'.

CHAPTER 14

Physical Development

'Mens sana in corpore sano'.[1]

The physical aspect of man is perhaps easier to understand than either the mental or emotional structures. Scientific and medical research over the last century has revealed a great deal about the performance and efficiency of the body and there is a wealth of information available. On the other hand, despite all the progress, not only is the physical aspect of man still incompletely understood, but there are considerable differences of opinion amongst experts concerning both the types and intensity of body conditioning, where this is to be felt essential for peak performance. Despite the information available, the man in the street who is keen to develop his physical abilities, may well be confused in his search for improved efficiency of action.

There are many people, of course, who see no point in any physical exercise beyond the minimum essential for modern living. This is an attitude of convenience and laziness rather than common sense. The dramatic increases within Western society of death by coronary heart disease for example, seem to be in no small measure due to unhealthy styles of living, and in particular a lack of regular exercise. Various research programmes both in America and Britain have shown that vigorous and regular exercise programmes can significantly reduce the incidence of coronary heart disease.[2] In 1976 a study was completed by the Sports Council, at the request of the Department of Health and Social Security, into the scientific evidence on the beneficial effects of exercise. The Council was sufficiently convinced by the evidence to begin its conclusion to its report,

> 'It is clear that exercise can be of considerable benefit to everyone both physically and mentally, and should be seen as a necessary element in the pattern of DAILY living at all ages'.[3]
> (my capitals)

Fortunately there now seems to be a distinct trend within our society for increased participation in both sport and outdoor recreation. Both in America[4] and Britain[5] there have been great increases in the numbers of people involved actively in these type of activities. Walking as a recreation is the major form of physical activity in both countries and the adventurous sports particularly have both grown and continue to expand in terms of popularity. Even the more extreme forms of physical activity are increasingly in demand. Along with the boom in jogging and orienteering, for example, has come the popularity of Long Distance Footpaths and marathon running. The New York marathon in 1972 attracted 284 starters. By 1982, ten years later, there were over 14,000 men and women entrants with two million watching the event live, as well as international television coverage.[6]

This significant increase in participation in physical exercise is to be applauded. It is to be hoped that it will progress to the point where all people in modern society participate, in some form or other, in sport or recreation on a regular basis – at least those with sedentary jobs. Like the mental and emotional aspects, the physical side of the human being will only function efficiently if it is used regularly. It will also only continue to grow and develop if it faces progressively more difficult challenges. The question as to whether it is worth making the effort implicit in such an approach can only be positively answered by experience. Those who engage in demanding physical activities and who have progressive and regular training, would tend to proclaim that their approach brings a great deal of enjoyment and satisfaction.

I would strongly support this viewpoint from personal experience. As a young man, rock climbing dominated my life. Weekends, vacations and summer evenings, my spare time was consumed in the fascination of Derbyshire gritstone and limestone and the crags of North Wales. After several years I had progressed to leading Very Severe comfortably but Hard Very Severe was giving me many problems. Several times I was either forced to retreat, or to realise I had reached the top of a route through luck rather than skill. My failure to progress was both frustrating and at times frightening. There were obviously weak links in both terms of movement skills and certain types of specialist fitness.

By chance, my build up of frustration coincided with taking a new teaching post at Wolverhampton (1961), which was both residential and provided a new gymnasium. At minimal expense I purchased some small nails suitable for brickwork and made about 200 small wooden blocks (1-2 inches long, ¼ inch thick and about ½ inch depth). I then hammered them in at random all around the walls up to about fifteen feet above the ground. What must have been one of the earliest and cheapest climbing walls was ready for use. In addition, the normal pull-out beams were inverted, and with a rucsac of progressively heavier weights, finger pull ups and traverses could be done.

This circuit of wall climbing and traversing, along with the work on the beams, was within one minute from my cottage on the school campus. For a whole winter it was used by myself and some of the boys almost daily, and sometimes even more frequently. I deliberately kept away from the crags during this period. When Spring arrived, I took a day on the Roches and Hen Cloud with one of the boys. I had hoped the training would show positive results. It did far more than that, for it brought me to understand that very hard regular physical work, by choice can bring both joy and exhilaration to eventual performance as well as satisfaction during the training. On that day a climb called The Sloth, previously too frightening to contemplate leading, proved most enjoyable, whilst almost all the hard routes on Hen Cloud succumbed although not without much respect for their pioneers.

The following weekend it was back to North Wales and the process was repeated. The first route was 'The Thing', which at that time had an awesome reputation as the hardest route in the Llanberis valley. Although it was so many years ago, I can still remember vividly, the enjoyment of that climb as I moved up a steep wall on very small holds feeling happy and completely at ease. For the first time in my life, my finger tips felt as strong as steel. Through the training I had moved up at least two standards in my climbing and greatly increased my self confidence and vitality. There were times in that year when I understood both the exhilaration of vertical rhythm and the real meaning of being a part of an inspiring environment.

The other experience that is perhaps worth mentioning with respect to development of physical skills and appropriate fitness, was many years later with regard to canoeing. I was very quickly made to realize that white water canoeing was as adventurous as rock climbing, only without running belays! Fortunately I was based in Manchester at the time and I had experts such as Ray Calverley and Ken Langford to show me that it was not quite as frightening as it first appeared. The progression to bigger rapids and bigger surf, along with the exploration of rivers in spate, continued over some years until the concept of journeys on the sea became very attractive. As leader of the Nordkapp expedition, a projected 500 mile journey with heavily laden kayaks to the most Northerly point in Europe in 1976, I was worried whether I could cope with the paddling demands. There did not seem to be a tradition of this type of expedition at that time and no-one consequently with whom to discuss likely problems, especially those of teno-synovitis of the wrist.

Remembering the method of achieving a personal breakthrough in my climbing I used Lake Windermere as a training facility. For almost six months I made time for paddling an average of at least fifty miles per week and where possible I would be out daily. As most of this work was solo and included winter conditions, with bitter cold at times and strong winds, I learnt both to build up a toleration to inclement conditions as well as the endurance required for expedition work. The expedition coincided with the worst summer in Arctic Norway since 1867 and my background training proved invaluable.

What I did not find generally on the expedition was the joy and exhilaration that can come from mastery of a journey skill. For much of the time the 500 miles of paddling was a question of hard work and combating muscular fatigue. It was only in later years that I eventually found the total rhythm I had been seeking. What had seemed a somewhat simple skill – forward paddling – turned out in practice, to be very complex.

In both my climbing and canoeing, progress had come through very regular and progressively more difficult training. Most of the training provided its own enjoyment and satisfaction with the stimulation of challenges ahead which would need a higher level of competence than I originally possessed. As these challenges were met, I felt not only that I had grown physically but that somehow I was both more mature, and more complete as a person.

When I reflect on 20 years of involvement with young people and trying to provide Physical Education, sport and adventurous activities for them, I feel saddened. Young people have both an instinct for adventure and a need to express themselves physically. Yet our traditions within education are that sport and outdoor pursuits are peripheral in terms of importance. In practice young people at school spend the bulk of their time at a desk. In latter years at secondary school for example, the amount of time formally in physical activity can be as low as five per cent, and is seldom more than ten per cent.[7] It is not uncommon for sixth formers to have no organised physical activity! There is no way that the physical growth of a young person can flourish with so little time devoted to it.

With physical growth and the development of motor skills and fitness, whether it is for a sport or an adventure journey, comes a sense of well-being. Self-confidence, and determination and other valuable human qualities can be developed to a high degree. Paradoxically the young person who has the opportunity to develop his talents in these activities can approach academic work in a more positive manner, compared to the young person who deliberately seeks minimal physical activity. The human being needs a balance of physical, emotional and mental experiences if he, or she, is to grow consistently towards his maximum potential. The 'feeling great' from physical activity, as a normal part of a lifestyle, tends to come from consistent effort in an activity of one's own choice. The degree of positive feeling tends to be directly in proportion to the amount of effort expended in progressively more difficult situations. With practice, normally over years, comes a deep form of relaxed concentration and the delight of the skills of the craftsman. In a sense the activity becomes a fundamental aspect of living that is immensely satisfying. The human being has a body that is designed to be used efficiently. The 'feeling great' that can come from rhythmic performance is potentially available to everyone. There is no lack of potential choice of physical activity except for the practical constraints, which are largely the result of a society that regards such activity as of minimal importance – at least in comparison to examinations. It is to be hoped that the unhappy growth in unemployment, along with the increasing degree of boredom and violence, vandalism and crime amongst the young, will accelerate the demand for more time and improved staffing for physical activities.

CHAPTER 15

The Natural Environment

There is a tendency for modern man to use the natural environment entirely for his own ends, and to be heedless of the consequences. This continual destruction of natural resources for material greed, could eventually lead to the destruction of mankind. Schumacher wrote,

'The continuation of scientific advance in the direction of ever-increasing violence, culminating in nuclear fission and moving on to nuclear fusion, is a prospect of terror threatening the abolition of man. Yet it is not written in the stars that this must be the direction. There is also a life-giving and life-enhancing possibility, the conscious exploration and cultivation of all relatively non-violent, harmonious, organic methods of co-operating with that enormous, wonderful, incomprehensible system of God-given nature, of which we are a part and which we have certainly not made ourselves'.[1]

This is a key statement. Modern materialistic society in particular, and the world in general, is in an appalling state. A radically different approach by the human race to its lifestyle, is essential if the world is to have a future worth living for. His latter comment that man is 'a part of Nature' is crucial in its implications. Modern man will glibly accept that he is part of Nature, then proceed to ignore the reality of what that means in practice. In his arrogance, he brings not only destruction upon Nature, but destruction upon himself. Happiness, which most people seek, was far more a condition of the 'simple' races around the earth, than a condition which could be ascribed to modern man. Spencer Chapman, who spent years in the less frequented parts of the world, discovered that of all people he had met, the really happy ones tended to be 'uncivilized people' – the Eskimos, the Herdsmen, the Aborigines. Whilst in the civilized world he thought the happiest tended to be those whose craft or technique brought them in touch

with the elements.[2] Among the simple tribes he discerned four sources for this happiness:
- A simplification of the objects of life
- A degree of companionship
- Beautiful surroundings
- Element of danger

Other travellers have found happiness a marked feature of some of the remote tribes of South America, Africa, and other regions of the world. In most cases, as soon as they were subjected to the influences of Western civilisation, then happiness tended to disappear rapidly.

If modern man is to find happiness, then he must accept the fact that, despite being an outstanding performer, he is only a tiny part of the natural stage. He will find this difficult, because of the modern tradition of arrogance and superiority over other forms of life. As Conrad so aptly remarked, through the butterfly collector in 'Lord Jim', who has come across a rare butterfly,

'. . . .Marvellous – look at the beauty – but that is nothing, look at the accuracy. The harmony and so fragile! and so strong! and so exact! This is nature, the balance of colossal forces. Every star is so, and every blade of grass stands so. And the mighty cosmos in perfect equilibrium produced this. Man is amazing but he is not a masterpiece. Perhaps the artist was a little mad! What do you think? Sometimes it seems to me that man is come where he is not wanted, where there is no place for him. For if not, why should he want all the place? Why should he run about here and there making a great noise about himself talking about the stars, disturbing the blades of grass'.[3]

Modern man must leave his arrogance behind, when he journeys in the outdoors. In its place should be humility, and as much awareness as possible. Although this may be most difficult in practice, it is worth the effort, because Nature holds the key to many of the problems of modern man. If he seeks happiness, then why should he not view this as an aim of all forms of life. This was the view of John Muir, who was vastly experienced in living with Nature,

'. . . .Nature's object in making animals and plants might possibly be first of all the happiness of each one of them, not the creation of all for the happiness of one. Why should man value himself as more than a small part of the one great unit of creation? And what creature of all that the Lord has taken the pains to make is not essential to the completeness of that unit – the cosmos? The universe would be incomplete without man, but it would also be incomplete without the smallest transmicroscopic creature that dwells beyond our conceitful eyes and knowledge'.[4]

The skylark would seem lyrically happy. Seabirds could be enjoying themselves as they perform their aerial acrobatics off the face of a cliff in a gale, or over a storm-tossed ocean. Technological advances have shown that some plants have some sort of feelings, in that they respond somehow to the presence of man. It is possible at least, that they also aspire to happiness. The humblest of men may grow and gather flowers. The greatest of men cannot create one.

The dolphins, like men, have a large cerebral cortex. Unlike modern men, these mammals are non-materialistic and non-aggressive. They have a reputation as 'happy' creatures and a tradition of making friends with fishermen and divers in the natural environment. Is it possible that they have developed happiness because they journey freely and are non-materialistic? It would appear that human restriction of their freedom can lead directly to their unhappiness. Three bottle-nosed dolphins, for example, at the National Aquarium in Baltimore were discovered by experts to have developed ulcers from too much work in an artificial situation. The Director of the Centre described their symptoms as both psychological and physical. They were given a drug commonly used to treat ulcers in humans and sent to a fenced-off bay in the Gulf of Mexico to relax for two months.[5]

Seals exhibit the curiosity which mankind rates so highly as an essential aspect of human intelligence. The look on the face of a seal at close quarters is almost human. It is hard not to believe also that seals too find happiness, as they play on a reef in an ocean swell.

To describe trees as having similar feelings seems very far fetched, and yet they certainly demand much more awareness and respect than is normally given them. On the Western slopes of the Sierra Nevada, for example, in Humbolt County live the tallest living things in the world. Here giant Redwoods grow up to 360 feet in height and are up to 2,200 years old. So self reliant are these trees, that fire is unlikely to do much damage because of the asbestos-like bark; and natural chemicals in the wood provide very effective protection against insects and fungi. Their roots seldom penetrate below six feet!

John Muir, to whom all trees were living things to be both

respected and revered, wrote of a particularly favourite dwarf pine tree. Growing at an altitude of 10,700 feet, and looking as though it could be plucked up by the roots, it was only about three feet high and 3½ inches in diameter. Yet that tree was 255 years old.[6] It is hard to appreciate the magnificent life of that tree – the exposure and the storms over such a long period.

Once one becomes AWARE, it is comparatively easy to have respect. The mountaineer soon learns to respect Nature, through the avalanches, rock falls, and storms. The sailor has the same feelings in very rough seas and menacing lee shores. Yet with the adventurer, partly through the demands of his specialism in terms of time, energy and concentration, and partly because of the arrogant feelings, that can so easily arrive after an achievement, there is a tendency to be both unaware and unconcerned about Nature generally and in particular, the abilities of other forms of life. Whilst it would be wrong to denigrate the great adventure and exploration achievements of mankind, they are seldom put into a natural perspective. All living things journey, and face dangers of many kinds in the process. An Arctic Tern, for example, travels approximately 25,000 miles annually, spends six months in the Antarctic and eight months of the year flying non-stop. The Willow Warbler (with a song of beauty and happiness?) which weighs only a few grammes, journeys 5,000 miles at the end of each summer. It has been calculated that equivalent human performance would be a journey of 24 million miles, or ten times the distance between the earth and the moon.

In the waters, similar astonishing journeys take place. All the eels in the rivers of Europe and North America are adults, yet they are all spawned in one particular area of the tropical Atlantic. Each one has to spend several years of travelling, in order to complete its development in fresh water.

The journeys of salmon are well documented. In order to reach their spawning grounds they have to be in prime physical condition. What are the feelings of the salmon, who, towards the end of a long journey, has to explode up a waterfall? What a magnificent achievement when he reaches his goal! And how sick I felt in my stomach when a red snapper I had caught when kayak fishing in Alaska, lay trapped under my deck elastics. Its thrashing around indicated its pain. I felt the pain and resolved never to fish again unless my survival depended upon it. What a change of attitude from all those times when I had felt exhilarated at catching fish!

How blind and arrogant a human being can be! I cannot make amends for what has happened but at least now I will try to keep to a complete minimum, my destruction of anything in the natural environment.

Like the salmon, birds apparently prepare for arduous journeys. The migrating bird lays down fatty tissue, which is used as a source of energy during the journey. The amount of fat is related to the total number of hours that the bird will fly without rest or food to reach its destination. As the human prepares for his arduous challenge, he might reflect that some other living things, are both totally self reliant and make extreme journeys without any need for modern technology! Apparently also, these other living things, 'tend to make the right decisions on the journey, otherwise migration behaviour would not have evolved.'[7]

In terms of skill also, the human being does not measure up too well in a natural perspective. The cheetah at 60mph would do well in the Olympics. The human equivalent of the power of the flea, is to jump unaided twice the height of St. Paul's cathedral. The Borneo gibbon does gymnastics through the trees with a joy and skill beyond those of Nadia Comaneci, whilst the Jesus Christ lizard walks on the water.[8]

My examples of the capabilities of other forms of life are only the tip of the iceberg. The more one learns of Nature, the more one realises how little one knows, and how incredible it is. Awe and wonder will develop as knowledge and awareness increase.

The human race rightly acknowledges the value of people helping each other in times of stress. This is again, not something that is solely their preserve. Hares have been observed trying to move the carcase of one of their kind.[9] Otters are reported to assist injured comrades by ranging themselves on either side. Elephants and ducks have also been observed doing the same thing. Compassion may be instinctive in living things. How else does one explain the cases of seals rescuing, or attempting to rescue, human beings, which has happened on several occasions with a variety of eye witnesses. Dolphins also can act in this way. In a recent case near the Cocos Islands in the Indian Ocean, an 11 year old boy, thrown off his surfboard into shark infested waters, was protected by a dolphin who swam round him for four hours.[10] Less dramatic but very common is the tradition that very young children alone on farms tend not to be harmed when in the thick of a group of animals such as cows and pigs.

Obviously there are links in terms of feelings, between human beings and other living forms.

My limited experience is confined to seabirds. There have been several occasions when I have been alone offshore in difficult breaking seas. At times, when I have felt very lonely and frightened, a fulmar or shearwater has glided by with a quizzical look at me. Each time I have felt some sort of indefinable psychological link with the bird. Its calmness and grace has had a marked effect on both my attitude and my paddling. Inwardly I salute its presence and carry on with the journey much more at ease with my environment. It has helped me in a moment of difficulty.

There are many classic examples in outdoor literature: the relationship of Joy Adamson with her lions over forty years, which led to three books which sold over 13 million copies; the incredible adventures of John Muir with his dog Stickeen, whose reactions could be described as human – fear, joy, terror and exhilaration in proportion to the experience.

In all these examples I have focused on specific aspects of Nature to try and make the reader aware of its wonders, and why we need to approach the outdoor environment with some humility. Paradoxically the deepest lessons of Nature are to be learnt by being aware of its TOTALITY.

Thoreau, for example, wrote of the need for man not to look at Nature directly, but through and beyond her.

By examining some of the writings of great outdoorsmen, and especially those who have journeyed or been alone in the wilderness, the relationship of the human being to Nature, in the deepest sense, can be seen. These quotations echo my own feelings. The eloquent writings of Muir, in the passage entitled 'The Sierra',

'Mountains holy as Sinaï. No mountains I know of are so alluring. None so hospitable, kindly, tenderly inspiring. It seems strange that everybody does not come at their call. They are given, like the Gospel, without money and with price.' 'Tis heaven alone that is given away.'

Here is calm so deep, grasses cease waving . . . Wonderful how completely everything in wild nature fits into us, as if truly part and parent of us. The sun shines not on us, but in us. The rivers flow not past but through us, thrilling, tingling, vibrating every fiber and cell of the substance of our bodies, making them glide and sing. The trees wave and the flowers bloom in our bodies as well as our souls, and every bird song, wind song, and tremendous storm song of the rocks in the heart of the mountains is our song, our very own, and sings our love.

The song of God, sounding on forever. So pure and sure and universal is the harmony, it matters not where we are, where we strike in on the wild lowland plains. We care to go to the mountains and on the mountains we care not to go to the plains. But as soon as we are absorbed in the harmony, plain, mountain, calm, storm, lilies and sequoias, forests and meads are only different strands of many-coloured Light – are one in the sunbeam.'[11]

The thoughts of the philosopher Alan Watts, on the sea,

Although the rhythm of the waves beats a kind of time, it is not clock or calendar time. It has no urgency. It happens to be timeless time. I know that I am listening to a rhythm which has been just the same for millions of years . . . It harmonizes with our breathing. It does not count our days . . . It is the breathing of eternity . . . .'.[12]

Nansen, stuck in the Polar ice for years, watches the winter night and speaks of,

'. . . the infinite cycle of eternity; such as Nature's everlasting rhythms'.[13]

and Muir, again,

'There are no harsh hard dividing lines in nature. Glaciers blend with the snow and the snow blends with the thin invisible breath of the sky. So there are no stiff, frigid, stony partition walls between us and heaven. There are blendings as immeasurable and untraceable as the edges of melting clouds. Eye hath not seen, nor ear heard, etc., is applicable here, for earth is partly heaven, and heaven earth.'[14]

Sir Martin Conway, in his book, 'The Alps' suggests that:–

'Nature after all, knows best and he is happiest who yields himself whether in the mountains or elsewhere, to perfect sympathy with her many moods'.[15]

Bernard Moittoissier writes in similar vein of the sea environment when on solo passage round the world. He mirrors my own feelings about personal kayak journeys off Scotland and in Alaska.

'The days go by, never monotonous. Even when they appear exactly alike they are never quite the same. That is what gives life at sea its special dimension, made up of contemplation and very simple contrasts. Sea, wind, calms, sun, cloud, porpoises, Peace and joy of being alive in harmony'.[16]

and later,

> 'My real log is written in the sky; it can't be photographed and given to others. It has gradually come to life out of all that has surrounded us for months . . . the silences, full of secret things between my boat and me'.[17]

Loren Eiseley experienced a similar harmony when despite being a non-swimmer and despite nearly drowning in his youth, he entered the river Platte in the Rockies, to float with it for an afternoon.

> 'Once in a lifetime, perhaps, one escapes the actual confines of the flesh. Once in a lifetime, if one is lucky, one so merges with sunlight and air and running water, that whole eons, the eons that mountains and deserts know, might pass in a single afternoon . . .
>
> . . . Then I lay back in a floating position that left my face to the sky, and shoved off. The sky wheeled over me. For an instant, as I bobbed into the main channel, I had the sensation of sliding down the vast tilted face of the continent . . . Moving with me, leaving its taste upon my mouth, and spouting under one in dancing springs of sand, was the immense body of the continent itself, flowing like the river was flowing, grain by grain, mountain by mountain, down to the sea . . .'.[18]

This particular journey superbly reflects the thoughts of the great American writer Thoreau, who emphasized that to love Nature meant an identification with it, a sort of mystical experience, a religion of the most fundamental type. 'In some sort, the end of life is that man should take up the universe into himself'.[19]

When one considers the threat of nuclear war, the anxiety and the mental illness within modern society. When one considers the millions of people killed and untold wars through the centuries on behalf of religious beliefs, it is easy to concur with Thoreau's statement:

'IN WILDERNESS IS THE PRESERVATION OF THE WORLD'.[20]

CHAPTER 16

The Holistic and Balanced Approach

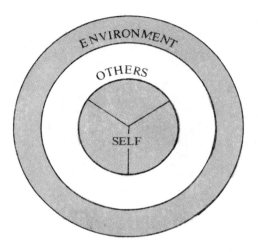

In looking at the basic sides of the human being in some detail, and especially the emotional and inner man, there is a considerable danger of ignoring the overall importance of seeing man as an entity. Analysis has a definite value in that it allows concentration and understanding of specific parts of life, but it must be balanced by synthesis – that aspect of the human brain which tends to be grossly underused. Synthesis may be defined as the putting together, especially of concepts, into a connected whole.

Modern man is conditioned through his education and his lifestyle to think and act in packages and specialities. In school he does a range of subjects which in practice are seen as separate, rather than interrelated. In later life also, he tends to package his activities into separate compartments within the general areas of work and leisure. This approach to life, whilst convenient, is counter-productive if he seeks happiness and maturation. Man is part of Nature and Nature does not recognise artificial divisions.

What is needed is a Gestalt or HOLISTIC view both of Nature generally and man in particular. The Gestalt view is, 'perceived organised whole, that is more than the sum of its parts'.[1] The first part of the definition seems to be acceptable common sense. In the case of the human being, it means that the emotions, mind, body and brain are all interrelated and cannot act independently. As Nietszche observed, 'We philosophers are not at liberty to separate soul and body; and we are still less at liberty to separate soul and spirit'.[2]

L. P. Jacks puts the case in the form of an analogy,

'We understand the wholeness of man as we understand the wholeness of a Beethoven symphony, not by hearing the instruments play one by one . . . but by hearing them play together, and so getting the wholeness of the music as it arises from the interactions of the separate contributions'.[3]

From the Eastern philosophies come similar thoughts. Yanagi notes that, 'Good work comes from the whole man, heart, head and hand in proper balance'.[4] Zen sees mind and body as two sides of one coin, whilst Fred Rohe in 'The Zen of Running', follows the same theme.

'. . . What is good for the body is good for the whole man. Our spirit is not separate from our body, any more than the water is separate from the stream. The water is the stream'.[5]

The second part of the definition of Gestalt as 'The whole being more than the sum of the parts', is much more difficult to comprehend, as it would seem illogical. Those who work on the frontiers of human ability however, might well acknowledge that there is something beyond logic. The more scientists discover, the more uncertainties they uncover. Nature is seen to be about balance and uncertainty. Those who adventure toward their outer limits similarly may experience something beyond normal understanding and somehow of deep significance.

Some personal experiences support this view. Two instances are still etched on my mind as being larger and more indefinable than what appeared to be the reality.

On the earlier occasion, two of us were returning from Holyhead to Barrow in Furness in a Shearwater catamaran – a completely open boat whose six foot square deck was like a table top about six inches above the sea (When it was calm!). Light and fluky winds had made progress very slow and by dusk, after 14 hours, we were still south of the entrance to Liverpool. As it happened, our crossing of the main channel to the port entrance, about ten miles offshore, coincided with High Water at Liverpool as well as darkness. The next hour was frightening. A myriad of both fixed navigation lights and the moving lights of large vessels lay ahead. We crossed over this main shipping lane, which seemed as busy as rush hour on a motorway, holding a handtorch, with flares at the ready. Our hearts were in our mouths. Somehow we got across, through the shipping, although at one time we were convinced that a large liner, lit like a christmas tree, was deliberately following our increasingly worried changes of direction. Eventually, after what seemed an age, we were across the shipping lanes and into an infrequented area of Morecambe Bay.

Mike, my crew, fatigued from the responsibility of 'collision-avoidance' navigation, lay under a bivvy sheet and slept. I was alone at the helm, and was to experience in the next two or three hours, something of almost magical and elusive quality which seemed to defy sensible analysis. The wind was up to about a force four from the east with a choppy sea. The 160 square foot of sail delighted in such a wind and we surfed northward at about ten knots. The night was clear, a large orange moon lit the sky and no other boats were visible. About 15 miles to the east the seafront lights of the coastal towns could be clearly seen. To complete the poetry every drop of spray over the boat, along with the wake, was phosphorescent. In practical terms I was sliding down the sea on a tray at speed in the dark, cold and fatigued, with an element of danger. In terms of feelings I was in a different world – a world of indescribable beauty that somehow opened a door to another more meaningful world. The cold grey dawn brought back the harsh realities of open boat sea crossings, but the memories of that night are as fresh as if it were yesterday.

Oddly enough the other experience which produced similar reactions was also in the Irish sea at night. Some years later, on a superb summer evening, I left the Cumbrian coast by kayak and headed west into the sunset. My destination was the Isle of Man, some forty miles offshore and somewhere beyond the horizon. The beach had been left with normal reactions of uncertainty and trepidation, relieved only by the coastguard, who, at the end of my phone call before leaving, had wished me luck. I had expected remonstration about solo kayaking to such a destination at night.

By midnight I was roughly 20 miles out and committed. Banks of sea fog could be discerned to the south, and a few stars above and to the west. The grey darkness revealed no form of life in any direction. I was alone and out of sight of land. Suddenly a bird fluttered close to my head and around the kayak. In those brief seconds my life and my feelings were transported and uplifted. With a deep interest in sea birds, I realized I was especially privileged to see a Storm Petrel, that tiniest of sea birds that somehow winters offshore and is seldom seen close to land. But it was far more than just seeing a new bird. It was a peak experience beyond my powers of description. The rest of the journey became unimportant, at least in terms of my feelings.

Both of these experiences were deeply concerned with beauty, and the heightened awareness that arises from exposed situations. To some extent also there was perhaps a natural balance in the situation between the performer and the environment.

The balance *within* the human being would appear also to be critically important both in terms of man's experiences and in his understanding of Nature. 'If we stretch a growing person out of shape by emphasizing too exclusive a development in only one sector of his personality, like the academic, we eventually create stresses in his personality that may interfere with continued growth in the over-emphasized sector'.[6] The over-emphasis on one aspect of mental development in formal western education is totally unbalanced and counter-productive to both personal development and a happier society.

Lance Lee discerns something of the problem,

'In the language of the Gestalt people, the peril courted by the non-doer, whose hand reaches only for the pen or the salad fork, is one of waking up distorted, unfulfilled and out of touch with the profound satisfactions of productive as well as creative accomplishment. There is a vital self-assurance factor in having done something which contributes to the physical well-being of self, family and community'.[7]

Alan Watts, the philosopher, would agree with this sentiment, 'After a long practice of something between Yoga and Zen Bhuddism style of meditation, I have at last come to see that there is nothing degrading or boring in soiling my hands'.[8] In reflecting on the immense problems of modern society, it would be worth noting the friction caused by the divisions into white and blue collar workers, those who administrate and those of 'lower status' who soil their hands.

This tendency to marked lack of balance within the lifestyle of the modern human being – the emphasis on one part of the brain and minimal physical and emotional involvement, contrasts very strongly with the adventure wilderness experience. As has been discussed in a previous chapter, the balance is a natural one. Contrasting emotions of fear and exhilaration are proportionately balanced. In turn these emotions are balanced against mental work under stress and the need for physical action. At the same time it is a holistic experience. This is a superb approach, both to Nature and to understanding oneself, especially within the distortions and complexities of the modern world.

In 'The Identity of Man', Bronowski stresses the fundamental importance of man being part of Nature. His studies had revealed that Nature was concerned with balance and uncertainty, as well as adventure.

'Nature is a network of happenings that do not unroll like a carpet into time but are intertwined between every part of the world; and we are amongst those parts. In this nexus, we cannot reach certainty because it is not there to be reached; it goes with the wrong model, and the certain answers ironically are the wrong answers.'[9]

The journey, then, that has a degree of uncertainty is a natural approach to life, as well as an acceptance that man himself, is part of a much greater scheme. Acceptance of this view, which is put forward by many eminent scientists and great men, requires some humility and tends not to be convenient to modern man. The perceptive writings of Aldous Huxley illustrate the point:

. . . 'In fact human individuals are not loose and separate and the only reason why we think they are is our own wrongly interpreted self-interest. We want to 'do what we damned well like', to have 'a good time', and no responsibilities. Consequently we find it convenient to be misled by the inadequacies of language, and to believe (not always of course but just when it suits us) that things, persons and events are as completely distinct and separate from one another as the words by means of which we think about them. The truth is, of course, that we are all organically related to God, to Nature and to our fellow-men. If every human being were constantly and consciously in a proper relationship with his divine, natural and social environments there would only be so much suffering as Creation makes inevitable. But actually most human beings are chronically in an improper relation to God, Nature and some at least of their fellows. The results of these wrong relationships are manifest on the social level as wars, revolution, exploitation and disorder; on the natural level, as

110

waste and exhaustion of irreplaceable resources; on the biological level, as degenerative diseases and the deterioration of racial stocks; and on the moral level, as an overweening bumptiousness; and on the spiritual level, as blindness to divine Reality, and complete ignorance of the reason and purpose of human existence.'[10]

These powerful sentiments would have been strongly supported by the outstanding Secretary to the United Nations – Dag Hammarskjold. The tremendous stresses on him as he sought to keep peace in a troubled world; the pressures of working up to twenty hours daily for weeks on end in times of crisis; and the loneliness of his job; led him to retreat into the natural environment for his sanity. He found the experience of Nature to be 'something extra-human' and the point of the experiences would be missed, 'unless we each find a way to chime in as one note to the organic whole.'[11] He went on,

> 'It is thus that in contemplation man discovers himself as inseparable from the cosmos as a whole . . . . If a human being is to have dignity, serenity and sanity, like a great tree, lion or galaxy, he must understand and feel that he is basically, this whole happening, and that his individual organism, is one of its innumerable gestures.'[12]

Much of Hammarskjold's writing has made a deep impression upon me, in part because of personal experiences. In 1981, inspired both by an expedition in 1979, and by the writings of John Muir, I returned to Alaska to attempt a northbound solo kayak journey from Sitka. I had left Britain with considerable reservations as to both how I would cope with such a journey and whether I could live alone for a summer with any real degree of enjoyment. The actual experience was unforgettable, but in a different way from what I had imagined. As someone to whom adventure had always seemed so crucially important, it was a surprise to find other memories that had more lasting significance.

These memories were of two kinds. The first was the awe-inspiring beauty of the Glacier Bay area: the swell of the Pacific ocean; the calving glaciers and icebergs; the mountains up to 16,000 feet. The solitude, wild life, and the pristine quality of the environment were breathtaking. To watch, for example, a humpback whale surface near icebergs in a beautiful dawn offshore, was unforgettable.

But it was perhaps the other memory that was more significant.

During the 600 mile journey I felt as if I were part of the ocean environment. I was almost totally content, feeling greatly privileged to be at one with such magnificence. In an indescribable sense, I was not alone, accepting fully that everything around me was somehow related to, and part of, me. It was the deepest feeling of peace and harmony.

These feelings were far stronger than the feelings of fatigue and indeed of fear. The last full day of the expedition, for example, was somewhat of an epic. By mid-evening I had travelled about 50 miles, been very frightened in thick sea mist off a coastline with no landings; with a fifteen foot swell and dangerous stretches of thick, floating beds of seaweed. It had been one of those days; the weather deteriorated until just before dark in a rising gale, I was off a headland in a rough sea that was exploding against uncharted reefs. I remained off the headland for something like ten minutes debating whether to turn back or go on. Despite fatigue and fear, deep down I felt at peace with my environment. Eventually I turned back, but there were no thoughts of defeat. I could defend the decision by emphasizing that it was common sense. Yet somehow defeat or conquest were both irrelevant. I was part of that ocean environment and that was all that mattered. Beneath my surface discomforts I was a contented traveller.

Interestingly for me, the land part of the expedition did not invoke quite the same feelings. A direct confrontation with a brown bear on a tiny island was extremely frightening, as I was both inexperienced in such encounters and carried no gun. I also knew that a bear had killed a local traveller in the area the previous year. There were few times on the expedition when I could either relax completely on land, or begin to feel that I was in complete harmony with all around me. No doubt if I had been an Indian, then this side of the expedition would have been less psychologically fraught. As it was, whilst I tried to have full awareness of bears and certainly had considerable respect for them, there was no way I could love them in such close proximity!

There are many who journey in the outdoors who express the underlying unity of all existence. Wordsworth, for example,

'I have felt
A presence that disturbs me with joy
Of elevated thoughts, a sense sublime
Of something far more deeply interfused
Whose dwelling is the light of setting suns

And the whole ocean and the living air
And the blue sky and in the mind of men
A motion and a spirit that impels
All thinking things, all objects of all thoughts
And rolls through all things'.[13]

And John Wyatt,

'True solitude is not loneliness. It is a great one-ness. One with everything: the cool grass, the deer, the glade, the wood, the countryside; this thin envelope of gas which gives our world life; the planet; the galaxy; the universe. It is not a loss; but a gift of wholeness. A wholeness with everything; a body, spirit, mind, and the whole level of attention. A wholeness in the one moment of time, poised in eternity'.[14]

On the bigger hills Frank Smythe reflects his experiences,

'Mountaineering is not one of those pursuits which can be evaluated in terms of achievement; it is a happy union between man and the universe a perfection of living and being'.[15]

While after untold ocean crossings in sailing boats, Moittoissier expresses similar feelings,

'. . . The wind, the calms, the fog, the sun are all the same, a single huge presence in which everything mingles and blends into a great light that is life.'[16]

To live then, is, as Rousseau wrote,

'to act, to make proper use of all our organs, our senses, our faculties, and all those parts of the human frame which contribute to the consciousness of our existence.'[17]

Life should be approached with a framework of values against which experiences can be evaluated, and the nature of further experiences decided upon. A simple framework would be:

To develop awareness of, respect for and love of SELF balanced against

a development of awareness of, respect and love for OTHERS balanced against

a development of awareness of, respect and love for the ENVIRONMENT.

If this framework can be used for all individual actions and if at the same time, this includes a genuine acceptance, in action as well as thought, of all the positive human virtues previously mentioned, then three things are likely to take place. First the individual is likely to develop his potential, mentally, physically, emotionally and spiritually to a very high degree, and thereby his maturity. Secondly his worth as a member of society is likely to be of a most positive and vital type. Finally he is likely to find satisfaction, if not happiness, as part of the vast unity of life.

CHAPTER 17

A Concept of Maturity

The simplest definitions of 'Maturity' refer to a state of perfect or complete development, or 'fully developed powers of body and mind'.[1] In other words, a human being becomes in fact, what he is potentially; what Maslow refers to as 'self-actualisation'.[2] In terms of the four basic sides used in this book, it would mean:

- full MENTAL development – of both right and left sides of the brain.
- full PHYSICAL development – which would seem to reach a peak comparatively early in life. However, there have been some remarkable physical feats by 60 and 70 year olds, especially in terms of endurance.
- full EMOTIONAL development
- full development of INNER MAN – the heart, soul, conscience or spirit.

This is an idealistic concept in that few men and women would appear to have reached all these goals. It is perhaps more a matter of being aware of how far one has travelled at any given point in time, with the knowledge and insight of where one is going; no certainty of how one is going to get there but determination to make every effort.

It is the emotional aspect and the development of inner man which seems both so complex and so fascinating in terms of what is seen as maturity. In particular, perhaps, is the question of the relevance of the positive human traits discussed in earlier chapters.

Young noted certain differences between mature and immature behaviour:

Marked increase in frustration tolerance
Decrease in frequency and intensity of emotional upset
Less impulsive and explosive behaviour
Reduction in degree of self-pity indulged in
Fewer signs of overt-emotional manifestations.[3]

If these differences are acceptable then the adventure experience strongly supports mature rather than immature behaviour. The control of the powerful emotion of fear is essential in a wilderness challenge. Similarly the qualities of Self-Discipline and Determination, along with the ability to put up with discomforts and hardships, are also highly relevant to the successful journey. The value of the same qualities is also seen in Hahn's Salem certificate (!) of Maturity with its

'capacity to endure hardships, to face dangers, a talent for organization; prudence; a fighting spirit; presence of mind; success in dealing with unexpected difficulties'.[4]

There are several other maturity factors in this definition, of which perhaps 'a talent for organisation' is the most interesting. As one grows, one becomes aware of the enormous difficulties of organizing one's own time in a balanced manner in terms of personal and social experiences. There always seems too much to do in the time available. This would seem pre-eminently a matter of integrity and self-discipline, associated with alert mental powers.

Huxley endorses the values of Self-Discipline, Determination, and Hard Work,

'It is by long obedience and hard work that the artist comes to unforced spontaneity and consummate mastery. Knowing that he can never create anything on his own account, out of the top layers so to speak, of his personal consciousness, he submits obediently to the workings of 'inspiration'; and knowing that the medium in which he works has its own self-nature, which must not be ignored or violently overridden, he makes himself its patient servant and, in this way, achieves perfect freedom of expression. But life is also an art, and the man who would become a consummate artist in living must follow, on all levels of his being, the same procedure as that by which the painter or the sculptor or any other craftsman comes to his own more limited perfection'.[5]

There is a strong suggestion here of the crucial value of Inner Man, that he must be directed by his heart or conscience, and not by intellect alone. In a sense this illustrates the importance of Self-Reliance, which is supported by Professor Meredith: 'Maturity is only for a few who achieve individuality and assert their responsibility.'[6]

He goes on to liken such people as being, of necessity, guerrilla fighters, within the context of modern society! Emerson also emphasizes the quality in his essay on Self-Reliance:

'Man is his own star; and the soul that can render an honest and perfect man, commands all light, all influence, all fate. Nothing to him falls early or too late.'[7]

This final sentence indicates another key quality already considered, that of Vitality. The ability to be optimistic and positive, concerning the problems of life would appear to be crucial. It is all too easy to be negative and pessimistic in times of stress. An emotionally mature person may well be one who accepts unpleasant facts whatever their origin, as concrete situations to be handled.

Professor Heath, on the other hand, stresses the value of Self-Confidence, 'Much evidence now indicates that the more in contrast to the less, mature person, has greater confidence in himself'.[8] Other thinkers lay the emphasis on humility as a key aspect. The ability to praise modestly, and to be able to accept criticism is one example. Many potentially great leaders in modern society have failed in this respect, displaying arrogance and intolerance at viewpoints different from their own. Carlyle wrote, 'The greatest of all faults is to be conscious of none.' Stekel, a psycho-analyst, puts the value of the trait in a different and unusual manner, 'The mark of the immature man is that he wants to die nobly for a cause, while the mark of the mature man is that he wants to live humbly for one.' In terms of examples, Mother Theresa is therefore exhibiting a higher degree of maturity than those humans who are famous for their noble deaths. At a less extreme level Robin Hodgkin wrote, '. . . to be an authority is to know how to doubt'.[9] There must be great temptations for experts to tend towards arrogance. Yet the paradox of life is such that the more expert a person becomes, the more he may realize how little in fact he knows. The validity of integrity as well as humility is obvious.

Compassion is another crucial factor. It seems a logical development of growth to begin life with 'please help me,' through 'I can take care of myself', to 'please let me help you'. The life of Nansen aptly illustrates the point. He worked enormously hard, in defiance of much criticism to raise the funds for his Fram expedition to the North Pole. The first part of that expedition was very much a case of everyone working together under his leadership. He then took off on a long and very demanding wilderness journey with another expedition member, in which self-reliance was a marked feature. After the expedition, which had stretched his resources to the limit, he eventually worked tirelessly for the League of Nations in the cause of peace. The former England cricketer David Shepherd, Bishop of Liverpool, and Lord Hunt of Everest fame [10] are more recent examples.

Courage, too, would appear to be a necessary ingredient. Professor Meredith puts forward the view that this quality and maturity are two sides of the same coin, both of which are dynamic and only endure by being kept on the move. He saw grave problems posed by the neurotic anxiety which tends to be characteristic of modern society. Indeed to such an extent that he noted that anxiety was incompatible with maturity.[11] This type of anxiousness should not be confused, however, with the normal healthy feelings of fear, which are so crucial to growth and understanding. In one sense to live with fear and not be afraid, can be seen as a final test of maturity.

The Bhuddists regard Maturity in a different way, although their most direct road needs the highest degree of courage. To them, the fully enlightened mind has three characteristic qualities:
–   Universal compassion
–   Wisdom that sees the true nature of reality
–   Skilful effective means to deal with all situations beneficially.[12]

St. Paul's perfect man has perhaps a similar enlightenment. His views were based on experiences of deep suffering. With him the fundamental quality of LOVE, which might be termed Compassion, includes nine elements:

Patience	Courtesy
Kindness	Unselfishness
Generosity	Good temper
Humility	Vitality
Sincerity	

In this list can be seen many of the qualities previously discussed. Vincent, writing in 1933, also sees the value of these qualities,

'The healthy personality . . . has vitality, courage and interest; alert, decisive, prompt direct, objective, resourceful, neat though not a slave to neatness, honest though not rude, humble though self-respectful, confident but not arrogant; it is kind, tolerant, reverent, is moderate in appetite . . . it appreciates its own strengths and its own weaknesses; it has a sense of proportion; a sense of humour, a love of beauty and a love of its fellow men.'[13]

Perhaps at the heart of maturity lies a very balanced person who has consistently both faced up to the truth about himself and consistently endeavoured to use his integrity. Truth can be seen to reside in the inmost soul of the person and integrity comes from INTEGRITAS, which means WHOLENESS. A lifestyle that aims to develop all the basic human aspects, including the key virtues, within a framework of awareness, respect and love for self, others and the environment is likely to lead to both maturity and 'wholeness'. To feel completeness as a free person, as a member of the human race, and as part of the unity of Nature, must be an incredible feeling. Saints and heroes must inspire the rest of the human race. To develop as a human being to this extent is to have complete empathy or attunement to all experiences. Significantly, whilst the most important journey is the journey inwards, the greatest mystics have often been great workers in the world, and have recognised their responsibility to give in service what they have received in contemplation. This is probably the basis for Eckhart's view that the highest form of lifestyle was that which combined CONTEMPLATION and ACTION.[14]

There can be no doubt that the true roads to maturity require the greatest effort and courage by the individual. He should take one of the roads with both confidence and humility,

'The human destiny is beyond our power to conceive. I believe we can travel toward that destiny without sacrificing intelligence, humour or compassion. If we can stay centred and balanced, we can take that journey in harmony with nature and other people. As for what a human being can do and be in this context, who would dare set the ultimate limits?'[15]

CHAPTER 18

In Pursuit of Happiness

The purpose of life seems to be towards certain absolute goals – Happiness, Wisdom, Truth, Freedom, Peace and Beauty. In some indefinable way these goals may well be synonymous with each other, and both difficult to attain as well as really understand. None of them perhaps are attainable as an end product or as a destination. Rather are they only realised through certain ways of 'living'. It could be argued that despite the great technological progress of modern man, these goals seem as distant as they have ever been in the history of mankind. If the aim of man is the greatest happiness for the greatest number then he has a very long journey ahead of him.

All the great religions of the world, both Eastern and Western have been concerned with the Truth, and have claimed that their's was the true faith. Yet millions have died throughout history as a result of religious wars. Perhaps because religions believe they have sorted out 'the Truth', they lack humility. The state of Northern Ireland might be a pertinent example. It would be tempting, therefore, to ignore religion in the future of mankind. That, however, is impossible, because the spiritual journey is the most important journey that man can make. He has to believe in the power of the truth and of the spirit, because the future of mankind depends upon it. Emerson is helpful in this difficult problem,

'We have our theory of life, our religion, our philosophy; and the event of each moment . . . are all tests to try our theory, the approximate result we call Truth, and reveals its defects. If I have renounced the search for Truth . . . joined some church or dogmatism . . . I am bankrupt. I have locked myself up and given the key to another'.

He puts a similar point in his essay on Self Reliance,

'Who so would be a man, be a nonconformist . . . nothing is at last sacred but the integrity of your mind . . . I am ashamed how easily we capitulàte to badges and names, to large societies and dead institutions . . . If we live truly we shall see truly . . .'.[1] Bhuddism has a similar stance,

'Be ye lamps unto yourselves
Be ye your own reliance
Hold the truth within yourself
As to the only lamp.'[2]

The modern writer Paul Johnson developed a set of new commandments. The Tenth was 'Never be deflected from the pursuit of Truth'.[3] If it appears to have been found, it is perhaps essential not to be dogmatic about the matter!

If truth is essentially an individual value then any society which believes that truth needs no more seeking has no interest in individual freedom. There has to be respect for the search for individual truth and dissent needs to be protected by justice. As far as is possible there has to be freedom of thought, speech and writing, movement and meetings.

In the individual search, the self-reliant journey in the outdoors may itself by a suitable, and perhaps highly favourable, path towards truth. As with any human quest, it would appear that the path should be approached with confidence and total sincerity. Frank Smythe takes it further,

'It is the immutable law of the Universe, that only through striving and suffering shall man learn to realize himself, to gain in awareness, to enlarge his moral stature, to discover truth and joy.'[4]

This emphasizes the need for the journey not only to be self-reliant, but also to be at stage III peak experience level for the individual. Kempis would agree 'A man's true qualities are revealed when things are difficult.' In other words, man learns the truth about himself from a challenging situation. If Schopenhauer's comment, 'Know thyself and know the world,' is accepted, then it can be seen that the future of mankind depends upon each individual tackling life as a personal challenging journey. A student leader endorses the personal search, 'There is no one truth in which the university can educate us. We have to find our own version of the truth for ourselves'.[5] Bhuddism would suggest that the journey is not only stage III but at the outer limits of personal capability,

'As long as life and death are seen as two phases of existence, then truth cannot be grasped'.

This would seem to be extreme stage III because the attitude of the adventurer would be to accept death as 'the last adventure'.[6] Those who eventually journey in situations of great objective dangers, perhaps, tend to recognise that death is part of that game. They have no intention of seeking death, and yet they are psychologically prepared to accept it as a distinct possibility. Tasker, for example, after epic climbs on Dunagiri and Changabang in the Himalayas, and after burying the dead from a nearby American expedition, wrote

'I was certain that I did not want to die but I knew that the risk in climbing gave its value. The sensation of being stretched to the limit mentally and physically was what gave me satisfaction and if there was danger it was another problem to solve, it made me more careful, made me perform at my best, and added a special uniqueness to the experience.'[7]

Such travellers are perhaps much nearer the truth of life than those with less courage.

There also appears to be an important link in this type of demanding journey between Truth and Wisdom. Alcman noted, 'Trial is the beginning of Wisdom', whilst Aeschylus also remarked that, 'Wisdom only comes through suffering'.[8] Both indicate the need for very demanding challenges within life. Wisdom would appear to be much more than the use of the intellect alone:

'. . . Ultimately intelligence and knowledge are poor – in fact dangerous – substitutes for wisdom.'[9]

The road to wisdom is, perhaps, by freedom in the presence of knowledge. That freedom is concerned with value judgements that stem from the heart or soul of man. The seat of wisdom lies in the heart, and is essentially a personal matter. Unlike knowledge, it is probably impossible to teach or communicate wisdom. Once one has found wisdom, however, it is possible to both live by it and do wonders through it.

As a Bhuddist monk emphasized in a lecture, wisdom is one of the two main energies of man. It is 'deep, insightful, incisive'. It is also regarded as one of the key elements of the 'fully enlightened mind.'[10]

It would seem both Truth and Wisdom can come from action in the most demanding of situations. 'Action should culminate in wisdom'.[11] Those who journey at the outer limits may be deliberately seeking both goals. It is more likely, however, that they are seeking Joy and Happiness from the experience. Nikki Lauda remarked,

'Everyone in racing knows the risk involved. If you're happy you
can handle the risk because the happiness is bigger than the risk.
But if you get bored then you think how risky it is; the freedom
you feel through your joy grows more and more limited.'[12]

Willi de Roos, after sailing alone round the world, and doing the
North West passage expressed a similar view,

'Happiness does not come from the absence of troubles but from
the ability to face them . . . Thus happiness has become
identified with action and ever more difficult action at that.'[13]

It would appear highly likely that Truth and Wisdom, Happiness
and Joy, are to a high degree, synonymous in these very positive
self-reliant stress situations. Within literally a few seconds, for
example, one can see the face of an athlete express intense suffering
which can then become extreme joy and happiness at the end of a
race. Similar expressions or feelings are common to all these type of
stress experiences, if they are of the stage III type rather than
misadventure.

Erich Fromm takes happiness a stage further,

'. . . happiness as well as unhappiness is more than a state of
mind. In fact happiness and unhappiness are expressions of the
state of the entire organism, of the total personality. Happiness is
conjunctive with an increase in vitality, intensity of feeling and
thinking and productiveness . . .'[14]

He goes on later, to write,

'Happiness is an achievement brought about by man's inner
productiveness and not a gift of the Gods. Happiness and joy . . .
are the accompaniment of all productive activity in thought,
feeling and action'.[15]

Anyone who has experienced these intense situations will know
the satisfaction from being totally involved – physically, mentally
and emotionally. Doug Scott, after a big wall climb wrote,

'I was thinking and feeling and experiencing all the elements of
joy and peace – like a man who has come down and out of his
L.S.D. trip I found the experience at first to be beyond words
. . . the climbers involved may experience a most lasting state of
heightened awareness and may even reach a truly visionary if not
mystical state of being.'[16]

Indeed the perfection of such moments are perhaps part of the
world of eternity.

The experience seems to be sufficiently powerful to take the
person out of normal time and space, and make him feel part of the

great entity of the world. It might be possible that this is a foretaste of the next development of mankind where 'knowledge' would be wordless and greater than at present. Professor Watts wrote,

'Ecstasy is a legitimate human need – as essential for mental and physical health as proper nutrition, vitamins, rest and recreation . . . At the peak of our technological affluences, these young people renounced the cherished values of western civiliztion – the values of property and status. Richness of experience they maintained, was far more important than things and money.'[17]

Although such experiences can be gained in a variety of ways, it would appear that they are most likely to occur in natural surroundings. Within those surroundings the solo wilderness experience may be the best medium, especially in conjunction with high mountains, oceans or deserts. What is of great importance to the future of modern society is that this type of experience is available to most young people. It need not be the preserve of the few well known adventurers.

In the complexity of modern living the simplicity of the outer journey is of profound importance. Sir George Trevelyan noted in his Wrekin Trust lecture [18] that the two ways to remedy the problems of the western world were the giving of tithe and a simplification of life. In the modern world 'simplicity' is seen perhaps in a derogatory fashion. That view is essentially one of either ignorance or convenience or both. Bertrand Russell had the view that the basic message of all great philosophers was essentially simple. Scientists too, try to work by reducing things to their simplest. 'It might even be maintained that the phenomena of the world and of Nature are relatively simple in terms of basic principles'.[19]

The importance of simplicity cannot be denied in terms of value, both in individual development and the future of the world. Fenelon saw real simplicity, so far from being foolish, as almost 'sublime'. For Frank Smythe, simplicity was the keynote of happiness. In contrast, complexity can be seen as a one way street. Seekers of the Truth as well as Happiness may look to Simplicity as a way forward. John Wyatt, in 'The Shining Levels', quotes an Indian professor friend,

'Europeans . . . accumulate too many 'Things' and pretend they are necessities. You Europeans are obsessed with Things. Your logic is obscured by the thought of Things. You no longer know the meaning of simplicity. And as truth is pure simplicity you can hardly recognise it. To find truth you need to give up everything. Truth is brought to the world by lonely men living simply in the wilderness'.[20]

Western man would appear to have largely lost touch with truth and beauty as a normal part of his experience. He only attains this state in occasional peaks. Adventure can help him back to the empathy with the world which is essential if he is to maintain this state as a normal part of life. Red Indian law is remarkably pertinent: western man is in search of truth, the Red Indian lives with truth.[21]

In an outdoor journey context, the advice is clear in that simplicity will often equate with efficiency. Paradoxically, simple life is extremely dependable on a high skills level, and may well require more courage and commitment. The climber, for example, who can solo a big mountain with the minimum of equipment, is much closer to truth and wisdom, happiness and freedom, than the large and complex expedition. In the same way, the sailor who can use as small a boat and as little equipment as possible, is likely to reap the most rewards from his efforts.

Many modern trends in adventure are in the opposite direction. The advantages of high technology, the 'ultimate' modern equipment and safety devices, tend to be used regardless of the effort and money required to develop them. Such effort and money, perhaps, should be used in helping solve the problems of the millions of the human race who are starving to death, or who are unemployed in increasing numbers. In the same way 'ultimate' adventures are devised which are often both outrageously expensive and often highly contrived. The media encourage these often bizzare expeditions as they make good copy. This style of adventure should be renounced, both because of the exorbitant costs and the selfish use of the resources of the world in both human and material terms, at a time when the human race is in a parlous state. Simple and inexpensive adventure has to be sought out. The individual is faced with the question as to whether he has sufficient courage and compassion to adventure in this manner.

If the European mountaineer must climb in the Himalayas then he should both journey and climb with minimal cost and equipment and the maximum of self reliance. The first visit to these mountains by Joe Tasker and Dick Renshaw and their subsequent ascent of a new route on Dunagiri would be a relevant example. In almost all senses this type of approach is to be preferred to large scale expeditions to Everest and other peaks. Messner and others have also emphasized the point by their simplicity of approach to formidable challenge.

In a different way but with the same principle, sea kayak expeditions from Europe for example, have no need to go to Cape Horn or Alaska. Impressive challenges exist in British waters such as a circumnavigation of St. Kilda from the Outer Hebrides, or the Faroes from North Scotland. Equally a Round-Britain sailing race could be accomplished by a fleet of Wayfarers at a fraction of the cost of the present fleets of highly expensive boats. The race might well take a great deal longer but the degree of adventure would be considerably higher, as well as infinitely cheaper. As a race it would also be markedly fairer! The same principle could also be applied to Trans-Atlantic and Round The World races. Boats could generally be considerably reduced in size and cost without detriment to seaworthiness, as some solo sailors have proved. Reductions in sophisticated equipment could also both improve the levels of self-reliance and adventure as well as reduce the cost involved.

With simplicity on the journey, there is likely to come Freedom. Freedom can be described as liberation from things and other people. The outdoor journey, if approached with simplicity as an ally, leaves behind as many things as possible. This begins to clear the way to Freedom. If the stage III adventure concept is accepted, and the person decides to take on as large a challenge as is consistent with his real potential, then he is much closer to Freedom. 'Inward freedom means that he finds strength to deal with everything that is hard in his lot, in such a way that it all helps to make him a deeper and more inward person, to purify him, and to keep him calm and peaceful'.[22] This is the core of freedom. Kierkegaard, a most remarkable philosopher, defined freedom not just as 'the goal of personality', but as, 'possibility'.[23] Freedom develops as man confronts his fear and moves ahead.

There could be no more powerful argument in favour of the self reliant wilderness journey at optimum levels of capability. The goals of life can be both experieced and expanded – Freedom – Happiness and Joy – Truth and Wisdom – Simplicity and Beauty.

Jonathan Livingstone Seagull points the way as he works desperately hard to develop his skills to peak performance levels in the face of adversity,

'. . . freedom is the very nature of his being . . . The only true law is that which leads to freedom'.[24]

By seeking perfect balance between one's aspirations and one's abilities, the first step is taken towards happiness and inward peace. 'SERENITY IS NOT FREEDOM FROM THE STORM BUT PEACE AMID THE STORM'.[25]

CHAPTER 19

The Universal Quest

If man can consciously strive to develop his physical, emotional and mental aspects in harmony with each other; if man can strive to be true to himself, and to accept the worth of the key positive human virtues; if, at the same time, he can base his actions in a balanced manner, between developing an awareness, respect and love for self, against similar feelings for others, and for the environment; he may then discover both an underlying and unifying aspect of profound importance. This is the spirit of BEAUTY, which can be seen as synonymous with Truth and Wisdom, Freedom and Happiness. The mark of a great man like St. Francis of Assisi, may have been that he could see and experience beauty to a much higher degree within himself, in other living things and in the environment, than a lesser person.

'Households, cities, countries and nations have enjoyed great happiness when a single individual has taken heed of the Good and Beautiful . . . Such men not only liberate themselves; they fill those they meet with a free mind'.[1]

The key to this concept lies, like so many of the problems of modern man, in Nature itself, because man is part of Nature. Whatever specific impulse takes man into the outdoor environment, there is the underlying feeling for its beauty

'No synonym for God is so perfect as Beauty. Whether as seen carving the lives of the mountains with glaciers, or gathering matter into stars, or planning the movements of water, or gardening – still all is Beauty!'[2]

Whilst accepting that such feelings are in the eye of the beholder, nevertheless, beauty is everywhere if it can be seen. In the words of the song, 'Everything is beautiful in its own way'. The feelings aroused by it are both intense and profound – awe and wonder, and a quality that defies analysis.

'If experience of beauty is pure, self-manifest, compounded

equally of joy and consciousness, free from admixture of any other perception, the very twin brother of mystical experience, and the very life of it is supersensuous wonder . . . It is enjoyed by those who are competent thereto, in identity, just as the form of God is itself the joy with which it is recognised'.[3]

They are feelings that are not uncommon among those who approach life with both awareness and humility:

'Who cannot recall . . . those silent instantaneous flashes of collusion with beauty of which even the memory so electrifies the emotions that no mental analysis of them is ever made. The intellect is knocked out in the first round. We can simply catalogue them without comment.'[4]

Many who have journeyed long in the great realms of Nature speak of profound experiences of beauty, synonymous with religion in its most fundamental sense. John Wyatt, for example, describes his feelings concerning a high view over Lakeland fells,

'I stood there for perhaps half an hour before I started back . . . It was as if I had been, by a divine choice, privileged to approach the golden gates of paradise. It left me breathless, elated, awed.'[5]

On the Pacific Ocean, Bernard Moittoissier, writes of the sea 'so beautiful it really breathes', and of his first view of the Southern Lights as 'the most beautiful thing I have ever seen' and 'perhaps this voyage's most precious gift to me'[6]

On the Atlantic Ocean, Van der Post, in the midst of a violent storm, is also deeply moved,

'The beauty of the sea and its accompaniment of wind was miraculous . . . It was . . . a moment of almost religious confrontation and experience of an assertion of ultimate truth that was an onslaught on all that was false in life and space and time.'[7]

Up in the wilds of Alaska, the explorer Robert Marshall writes of a brilliant day,

'. . . We felt genuine exultation in seeing the flawless white of those summits and the flawless blue of the sky . . .'[8]

Whilst further South in Colorado, John Muir is similarly inspired by the morning after a severe storm,

'In vain as I crossed the open meadow did I search for some special palpable piece of beauty on which to rest my gaze . . . But no such resting-place appeared in the completed heaven of winter perfection . . . It is all one finished unit of divine beauty, weighed in the celestial balances and found perfect.'[9]

Up in the Polar region Nansen and his crew watch the Northern Lights. They make a profound impression,

'No words can depict the glory that met our eyes . . . surpassing anything that one can dream' and 'reaching such a climax that one's breath was taken away.'[10]

Volumes could be written of those who have experienced the beauty of Nature, from the tiniest flower to the view of earth from outer space. John Muir perhaps captures the magic of all such experience,

'These beautiful days must enrich all my life. They do not exist as mere pictures – maps hung upon the walls of memory to brighten at times when touched by association or will, only to sink again like a landscape in the dark; but they saturate themselves into every part of the body and live as always.'[11]

In these examples man is looking outward and demonstrating his love for the environment. There is no mention of conquering Nature. Such a thought would seem ridiculous to such people – as ugly as Nature is beautiful. But what of those who apparently do go out to conquer the mountains, oceans and deserts at their most formidable? At first sight it would appear that they are not fundamentally concerned with beauty but with conquest. Although for the young and immature this is in one sense true, even at this level the importance of beauty is fundamental. It is essentially the 'feeling great' from overcoming a difficult challenge that is a feeling of beauty. The reaction of 'that was great' is synonymous with 'that was beautiful'. As G. W. Young acutely observed,

'It is when physical strength and endurance have been tried to their utmost that we become sensitivized to beauty, and aware of deeper emotional possibilities in ourselves.'[12]

This awareness of self leading to a deeper acceptance and respect for self, providing that it is not allied to arrogance, is eminently acceptable. In other words love of self is justifiable providing humility is present, and the implied awareness, respect and love is also extended to all other forms of life and the natural environment generally. The young climber, canoeist and other types of specialists in the outdoors can be singularly blind in both their awareness and responsibilities, as part of a great entity. In the enthusiasm of the specialism and the emphasis on urgency and speed, and with success being seen by the results, rather than by how one feels, a fundamental value of the experience may be missed.

As a young climber for example I must have been particularly unaware of the beauty of the outdoors, at least in a conscious sense. Rather was it the escape from the city, the joy of the physical challenge, and the success in the number and difficulty of the climbs, that seemed important. Only once as an adolescent climber do I remember being awestruck by beauty. I had taken a day off school and hitched up to Gardom's Edge in Derbyshire. In the early evening after running out of energy, I sat on a prow of rock above the valley and watched the sunset. So splendid was the sunset that all the gritstone was suffused in a warm pink. I was deeply impressed.

What was perhaps significant in this incident was that I was in a contented frame of mind having finished climbing, and I was alone. An occurrence in Arctic Norway had a not dissimilar background. The climbing expedition had finished, and I lay content in my sleeping bag in the heather beneath the stars. As I was musing over the long hitchhike to Bergen the following day, the sky suddenly became alive with shimmering curtains of varying colours and shapes. I watched spellbound for several hours, far too excited to sleep. It was September and I had witnessed a display of the Northern Lights.

Much later in life I became much more receptive to Beauty through journeying in tiny boats on the sea. Perhaps the activity allowed more time for visual awareness than climbing. Perhaps I was more in harmony with the sea than the mountains in some deep psychological sense. Perhaps above all I was much older and both more mature and more aware of the environment. At all events, areas such as the islands off the West and North coasts of Scotland seemed to possess an infinite variety of compelling beauty, whether it was the sea or the clouds, the hills or the flowers and wildlife. Journeying, often alone, at dawn and dusk, I seemed to find beauty almost everywhere.

The small scale of Scotland in no way detracted from the immensity of its beauty. It may even have enhanced it. Alaska in contrast, impressed its beauty upon me by its grandeur. The magnificence of its wilderness was accentuated by the lack of people, and the blending of huge forests and high mountains, with the purity of the Pacific Ocean. My awareness was perhaps increased by long days of effort in a kayak. This likelihood was emphasized when, after the 1979 expedition, we retraced some of our kayak journey on board a modern ferry en route for Seattle. If anything, the views from the ferry should have been superior to those from the deck of a kayak, which is so close to the water. In terms of feelings the opposite was true. The ferry journey left no deep feelings of beauty. This modern method of journeying – viewing Nature through a glass window with no physical effort involved – cut me off completely from being part of that environment. I have found the same reaction in aeroplane travel. The views at times are outstanding and yet I have never experienced the deep feelings one might expect from such beauty. I am psychologically removed from it by an air-conditioned cabin and have to make no effort to be in that place, except for the purchase of a ticket!

It would seem that appreciation of beauty in the outdoors may develop as one becomes more experienced, providing that the activity is largely self-reliant and demands physical effort. Frank Smythe for example wrote,

'Because I was older and more susceptible to impressions, my first view of the hills of Wales taught me more than anything I had seen seven years previously in Switzerland'[13]

Smythe was a mature mountaineer, whose mountaineering was really a search for beauty – within himself in terms of his feelings, when he had successfully overcome some difficult challenge – as well as with the mountain environment.

Such an approach, however, need not be the prerogative of those with extensive experience. Prunella Stack for example, who as a beginner climbed South Crack on Inaccessible Pinnacle on Skye, has an excellent description of the link between awareness of beauty and personal effort,

'The reward of such climbs is the stretching of one's powers to their fullest limit. The catharsis which the effort, mental and physical, entails also brings an awareness of beauty which seems unique. When the world had stopped revolving I realized that I was now part of this mountain scene in a new way. I had earned my place there, I could identify with the texture of the rock and the sweep of the face; the mountains would disclose for me their private beauties of the crag, crest and ledge, unknown to those who never climbed into their midst'.[14]

If one turns to sport, that man-made substitute for the adventurous journey, beauty and its key importance can still just about be discerned. The athlete trains for peak performance. When he gives of his best, he may well have a peak experience – feelings of joy and exhilaration in expressing himself at the outer edge of his limits. The problem with competitive sport is that far too often the performer and his coaches are concerned to win at all costs, and to judge 'success' solely by results. With this naive and arrogant approach to life, sportsmanship tends to disappear, especially when money and status are held to be of vital importance. Instead of feelings of beauty emerging from the experiences, there tends to be a great deal of ugliness and recrimination. Sordid behaviour by international sportsmen, for example, is a typical aspect of modern society. The performer has to be sufficiently mature to realise that, in essence, he is competing against himself – his strong will against his weaker will. With this attitude, which accepts that competition with others is in one sense meaningless because of the uniqueness of the individual, then the peak experience can come at any time, whatever his result, and even during training. By accepting competition as a tool rather than an aim in itself, he can develop an expending awareness, respect and love for self, with reactions of 'feeling great' and 'that was beautiful'. In 1979, for example, Alderman tested 136 Canadian athletes and found, 'Male athletes showed a surprising strength of attitude towards physical activity as an aesthetic experience'.[15] The joy of effort is one essentially of beauty through balanced demands on the physical, emotional and mental aspects. In place of the fear of falling off the mountain, is the uncertainty of how far the body can be extended before there is collapse. The discovery that the frontiers of possibility can be extended is magnificent, especially if the person realizes that it is the effort that counts, and that the immediate goal is to reach his own outer limits, regardless of others.

The analogy between sport and the outdoor journey in terms of the concept of beauty can be taken significantly further. Apart from self-development, there is the development of respect and love for others. The relationships between people in a team, whether on a mountain or in the sporting arena, can be developed to extremely intensive levels in psychological terms. Friendships can become so strong that they are something of great beauty, and again really beyond description. In exceptional circumstances, the combined performance of two teams, as well as of individual performers, can be so magnificent that the entire audience can be caught up in a peak experience. The whole situation can become something of great beauty, indelibly printed on the minds of all those involved.

Such experiences, of course, are neither confined to adventure in the outdoors nor to sport. They can happen in any situation where people are involved. Concerts and festivals are perhaps particular examples. In all of them however, there is something of great beauty involved and an experience to be treasured.

The need for receptivity to Beauty, indeed its acceptance as a fundamental approach to living, has never been more important than in the modern world. The present order of society does not recognise Truth and Beauty and apart from occasional flashes, both have become strangers. Beauty is innate in all forms of life and it can be seen as the basis for culture. Almost everyone reveres beauty no matter what may be his cultural background. High intelligence and advanced techniques are not essential. A human being, through his hands, can produce something of great beauty, at least in his own mind's eye, if it has been inspired from his heart and demanded all his abilities. Similarly, if approached with awareness and humility, feelings of happiness and beauty can be experienced in relationships with others, with their creations and achievements and in helping them when they are in need. At the same time, there is the happiness and beauty available through creation. As Thoreau indicated in the 1890's, human existence should not be a duty or a burden, not a means to an end, but a self-justifying aesthetic joy.

Nature was not, in the words of Frank Smythe,

'a thing apart, something to be stormed and conquered, it is a part of us, an all-prevailing beauty and magnificence in which we strive to realize ourselves and in realizing, learn the true importance of existence'.[16]

In the final analysis is the beauty of the entire harmony of everything. In the darkest days of Dag Hammarskjold's struggles to sort out the strife of the modern world, he wrote,

'When the sense of the earth unites with the sense of one's body, one becomes earth of the earth, a plant among plants, an animal born from the soil and fertilizing it. In this union, the body is confirmed in its pantheism.'[17]

Nature is a universal harmony, in which forces great and small collaborate to create beauty. The interplay between all living things and their natural surroundings provide each with the opportunity to find happiness during its time on earth.

****

If young people are to begin to see the values of beauty and of life beyond materialism. If young people are to begin to discern that they are part of Nature with all its implications. If young people are to begin to understand their responsibilities as part of the human race, then they must be given every opportunity to adventure in the natural environment. In return they will bring great benefits to society through their increased maturity.

To climb, sail, canoe, or journey in a hazardous environment in a self-reliant manner, may seem a dangerous and unjustifiable extravagance in a modern world. Nothing could be further from the truth, for life is a paradox. Society desperately needs young people who are determined and courageous. Young people are the most valuable resource in the world – the citizens of tomorrow. When they go on a demanding outdoor journey they are displaying the exploring instinct common to all living things. And in common with all other forms of life on the planet it is both natural and traditional for that journey to be dangerous and uncertain.

There can be no doubt that young people, if efficiently trained can be extremely capable and self-reliant.

The wilderness journey can teach them something of the universal values basic to the development of the human race. It can give them self-confidence, self-respect and self-discipline. It can give them an appreciation of the values of humility, integrity, and the need to be both very determined and to work hard if they seek lasting satisfaction from any lifestyle. At the same time it can teach them the necessity to work together and the need to regard to life other than from a purely selfish standpoint. Finally it can begin to make them aware of the natural environment, the need to protect it, and hopefully to learn to love it.

The modern bureaucrat who defines progress as increased security and greater ease of living, attempts to inhibit these adventurous journeys by the young
- by keeping outdoor pursuits as peripheral and unimportant in comparison to the 'real' education of school lessons.
- by avoiding the term 'adventure' and emphasizing instead the respectability of 'Outdoor Education'.
- by masses of safety regulations, procedures and qualifications.
- by emphasizing the importance of 'the residential experience' rather than the 'adventure' experience.
- by taking undue heed of the unbalanced sensationalism shown by the media when serious accidents happen to young people in the outdoors.

Petty restrictions and negative attitudes will lead both to young people seeking anti-social forms of adventure, and to them working directly against making society a better place to live in. Such restrictions are the work of those who have no concept of the importance of adventure to society in general, and yet who are prepared to allow adolescents to engage in battle for their country.

Alfred Whitehead would have strongly supported this view. As a Fellow of Cambridge and Professor of Philosophy at Harvard University his work included the study of civilizations. He was convinced that any civilized society exhibited five crucial characteristics: TRUTH; BEAUTY; ART; PEACE; and ADVENTURE. Of the latter, he wrote.

'A race preserves its vigour so long as it harbours a real contrast between what has been and what may be; and so long as it is nerved by the vigour to adventure beyond the safeties of the past. Without adventure civilization is in full decay.'[18]

APPENDIX A

Safety Principles

The first law of the animal world is 'Know where you are and what is around you.' The first rule of safety, similarly may be termed as:

AWARENESS

The second rule might be termed:

APPROPRIATE ACTION IN THE EVENT OF DANGER

Safety regulations for each activity tend not to cover all aspects, and by their nature, to be restrictive. Where they try to cover all eventualities, they are both lengthy and difficult to absorb. Far too often they are also written as an insurance cover, rather than with the aim of making young people self-reliant and all that this implies.

Safety principles which should apply to *all* the activities are easier both to read and absorb. Where the principle does not apply, then the teacher should be even more on the alert. The following list is probably not comprehensive, but it may be helpful. All the principles would seem to be important, as the outdoors has the uncanny knack of finding the weakness when the luck is against you.

1. Accept responsibility for the safety and the well-being of all party members the whole time.
2. Accept that work in dangerous situations with young people has
   (i)   to be justified beforehand
   (ii)   to be PROGRESSIVE
3. Know that most accidents are avoidable.
4. Never presume that all the answers are known.
5. Know that success in overcoming a dangerous situation should be more the result of careful planning and appropriate action rather than luck.
6. Be inwardly pessimistic (awareness) and plan accordingly. Be outwardly optimistic when necessary.

7. Be especially aware of the dangers possible in the so-called 'low risk' activities; and those possible after the surmounting of the apparent crux of the journey.
8. Always work well within personal limitations of fitness, experience and ability.
9. Understand different types and degrees of danger – in broad subjective terms and in relevant technical detail.
10. Have general awareness of the stages of adventure – especially the need to normally avoid misadventure.
11. Know the particular environment before using it with young people. Never take even local terrain, or apparently easy situations, for granted.
12. Know that there are some days when some outdoor conditions, especially in winter, are too dangerous for most young people.
13. Know the implications of the weather forecast if this can produce danger in the activity.
14. Plan carefully, but accept flexibility in the programme, as both party members and the outdoors are dynamic.
15. Know the group, the back-up resources, and how to use them.
16. Use appropriate party equipment efficiently, and ensure the personal leader equipment is efficient. Know the limitations of all basic and emergency equipment.
17. In all training leading towards self-reliance, ensure all basic skills are efficient by testing in controlled situations. These should include efficient emergency skills.
18. Ensure, where approriate, that party members know the value of self-reliance.
19. Accept that THE STRENGTH OF A CHAIN IS IN ITS WEAKEST LINK. (Incidents in the outdoors are generally the result of a weakness, or several of them, be it in an equipment item, lack of a skill, or a personality factor.)

IMMEDIATELY PRIOR TO THE JOURNEY
1. Explain the nature of the journey and procedures.
2. Careful explanation of all the basic safety aspects.
3. Explain communications.
4. Check procedure for links with emergency resource.

DURING THE EXPERIENCE
1. Have complete concentration and awareness at all dangerous

times. (This is often extremely difficult in practice and requires prolonged training.)
2. See all the group all the time.
3. Have an effective communication system.
4. Do any challenge first if it could present unacceptable danger to a party member.
5. Never leave beginners alone and unattended in potentially hazardous areas.
6. As leader be in the place where you are most needed (e.g. placing yourself between the danger and the party member; or if this is impossible, then in the best rescue position). Use a buddy system and helpers in most efficient manner.

AFTER THE EXPERIENCE

Evaluate the experiences carefully and systematically against the stages of adventure, and the safety principles.

Bibliography & Notes

INTRODUCTION

1. December 1969. Those present included P.E. Advisers, Centre Wardens, Instructors, Teachers and Lecturers.

2. There seemed a tendency at that time for some Centre work with young people to be more of a holiday than any attempt to provide them with adventure. The holiday approach was both much easier for staff and seemed to debase the adventure concept.

3. Established in October 1970 at the Woodlands Centre.

4. It would seem likely that a considerable number of those in positions of responsibility in Outdoor Education within the state system of education, including Inspectors, Wardens and Advisers, had no in-depth experience of personal adventure. If there had been such experience, it is hard not to believe that the adventure concept would have progressed much more in Britain in the last twenty years. There are a significant number of British instructors who have become so frustrated with the lack of adventure in British Outdoor Education, that they have gone to work abroad, especially in USA, Canada, Australia and New Zealand.

5. The Ambleside Area Adventure Association established in 1977.

6. Advanced Certificate in Outdoor Education. A One Year In-Service Course at Charlotte Mason College, Cumbria, that developed the theory and practice of Adventure Education, 1976-1982.

7. The progress of these youngsters has depended on close liaison and cooperation with parents and the headmaster.

8. Easter and summer expeditions round the Isle of Man, Coll and Tiree, Iona, and parts of the Outer Hebrides and Orkneys.

9. As 6 above.

10. Held at the Queensland Outdoor Centre, near Brisbane, September 1981. Extract from keynote speech on *The State of Western Society & its Education Systems* reprinted in The Journal of Adventure Education No. 5.

11. See *A. Solzhenitsyn Speaks to the West;* The Bodley Head 1978.

12. See 9, above.

13. Well-known examples include the Findhorn Community in North Scotland and the Centre for Alternate Technology at Machynllech in Wales.
    There are many other small groups and organisations. For details see article, Orgill R., *Adventure into Alternatives*, Journal of Adventure Education No. 3 1981.

14. Unlike the major political parties in Western Europe, the Green Movement is politically more attuned to the human race living in harmony with the natural environment, with an emphasis on 'small is beautiful'; non-nuclear forms of energy and a pollution tax. It is particularly strong in

West Germany where Petra Kelly, a former leader of the movement has attracted international attention. Membership of the movement is over a quarter of a million in Germany with people from all walks of life. The British equivalent is the Ecology Party.

CHAPTER TWO:
SKILLS LEARNING
1. The Corner, Clogwyn Du'r Arddu. in 1960
2. The Vrwyny gorge in the winter of 1965.
3. The Inner Game Ltd., 200A West End Lane, London NW6 1SG.
4. The Sporting Bodymind., 115 St. Mary's Mansions, St. Mary's Terrace, London W2.

CHAPTER THREE: SAFETY
1. Quotation, Argus Posters.
2. See Safety Principles, Appendix A.

CHAPTER FIVE:–
MISADVENTURE
1. 1959.
2. Service R., *More Selected Verse*, p. 1; Dodd, Mead & Co. (N.Y.) 1960.
3. Smythe F. S., *The Spirit of the Hills*, p. 269-286; Hodder & Stoughton 1940.
4. Worsley F. A., *Shackleton's Boat Journey*, p. 121; The Folio Society 1974.
5. Hammarskjold D., *Markings*, p. 136; Faber & Faber 1964.
6. Teale E. W., *The Wilderness World of John Muir*, p. 322; Houghton Mifflin Co. (Boston, USA) 1954.

CHAPTER SIX: THE
INSTINCT FOR ADVENTURE
1. Article by Mortimer J. on *Enoch Powell*; The Sunday Times 18.11.79.

2. The lack of enthusiasm for Field Studies was partly due both to the traditional methods of teaching that were used and to a lack of expertise within the staff. Even with modern techniques and gifted teachers, however, it would seem unlikely that Field Studies would ever be as popular as adventure activities for most young people.
3. An unfortunate result of the popularity of gorge walking has been the destruction of the flora, including rare species, especially in North Wales and the Lakes. It is essential that group leaders are aware of their responsibilities in terms of preservation of the environment, even if this means some restrictions of an adventure activity.
4. Hillaby J., *Journey through Britain* pp. 203-27; Constable 1968.
5. Article, *The Great Outdoors*; Sept. 1982; vol. 5, No. 9.
6. BBC TV programme on American Theme Parks 3.2.80.
7. BBC TV programme on Pleasure Parks and Roller Coasters 1979.
8. Business News, The Sunday Times 4.10.81.
9. It is also very noticeable that there are several major and a myriad of minor commercial organisations that offer adventure holidays to the younger generation. These packages of adventure are often staffed by inadequately experienced young people who tend to be paid at minimal rates. Capitalizing on the instinct for adventure in the young can obviously be very profitable but the educational value of such packages are likely to be severely limited.
10. Pringle K. M., *The Roots of Violence & Vandalism* p. 5; National Children's Bureau 1973.
11. Dr. Rosenthal S. R. article *The Fear Factor* p. 61 *Sport & Leisure*, Sept. 1982; The Sports Council,

London.

12. Cousteau J., article *The Impulse to Explore*; The Saturday Review, New York 1976.

13. Dr. Baker R., *The Mystery of Migration* p. 30; Harrow House Editions Ltd., London 1980.

CHAPTER SEVEN: TOWARDS THE DEVELOPMENT OF A PHILOSOPHY

1. Russell T. & P., *On the Loose*; Sierra Club Pblk. Library 1979.

2. The Concise Oxford Dictionary, p. 626; 7th Ed. 1982; OUP.

CHAPTER EIGHT: SELF-DEVELOPMENT – GENERAL

1. Schopenhauer.

2. An interesting comparison with Drama can be made with the nervousness of the performer in front of the audience. In comparison to the outdoor journey, however, it is a contrived rather than a natural experience.

CHAPTER NINE: MENTAL DEVELOPMENT

1. Smythe F. S., *The Spirit of the Hills*, p. 209; Hodder & Stoughton 1940.

2. Huxley A., *The Perennial Philosophy*, p. 152; Fontana 1959.

3. Prof. Whitehead A. N., *The Aims of Education*; Benn Pbk.

4. Post L. V. D., *The Lost World of the Kalahari* p. 61; Hogarth 1961.

5. My comments on the brain are grossly simplified. The brain has a front, middle and back, as well as left and right sides. All these aspects, however, would appear to be integrated within the adventure experience.

6. Dr. Hemming D., *The Betrayal of Youth* p. 36; Marion Boyars 1980.

7. Koestler A., *Act of Creation*; Hutchinson 1976.

8. Cousteau J., article *The Impulse to Explore*; The Saturday Review 1976.

9. Quoted in Dr. Hemming D., *The Betrayal of Youth* p. 20; Marion Boyars 1980.

10. De Bono E., *The Mechanism of the Mind*; Penguin 1971. His concept has been applied by the government of Venezuela.

11. H.R.H. The Duke of Edinburgh – extract of speech at press conference at 20th Birthday Celebrations of the Duke of Edinburgh Award Scheme. Quoted in the 1976 Annual Report of the Scheme.

12. Prof. Fromm, E. – comment from BBC TV programme 1980.

13. Jalal-Uddin-Rumi – quoted in Huxley A., *The Perennial Philosophy* p. 149; Fontana 1959.

CHAPTER TEN: EMOTIONAL DEVELOPMENT

1. How far a trait, quality or any other aspect of the human being can be developed through experience will ultimately depend upon the innate or inherent degree of that aspect within the person concerned. In almost all cases, however, there would seem to be considerable scope for development.

2. Definition in a letter from Mr. K. Stevenson to the author.

3. Nietzsche F., *The Portable Nietzsche* p. 682; Viking Press (N.Y.) 1964.

4. Fairfax J., *Oars across the Pacific* intro.; Kimber Press 1974.

5. Cundy R., *Beacon Six* p. 248; Eyre & Spottiswoode 1970.

6. Harrer H., *The White Spider*; Hart Davis.

7. Schweitzer A., *My Life & Thoughts* p. 257; trans Campion C. T.; G. Allen & Unwin 1933.

8. Rolland R., *Michelangelo*; 1915 (N.Y.); quoted in May. R., *The Meaning of Anxiety* p. 182; W. W. norton (N.Y.).

9. Emerson R. W., *Essays*; Allinson W. M. 1841 (N.Y.).

10. Mulville F., article *Iskra comes*

Home; *Yachts & Yachting*
29.1.83.

CHAPTER ELEVEN:
VITALITY & INTEGRITY
1. Emerson R. W., *Circles; Essays;
   First Series*; 1841.
2. Vauvenargues *Reflections &
   Maxims*; trans. Stevens F. G.
3. McFee W., *Casuals of the Sea*;
   1916.
4. Huxley E., *Scott of the Antarctic* p.
   117; Pan Books 1979.
5. Shakespeare W., *Hamlet*.
6. Prof. Fromm, E., BBC TV
   interview 1978.
7. Dr. Humphrey N., *Bronowski
   Memorial Lecture*; quoted in The
   Listener 29.10.81, p. 493.
8. Yanagi, *The Unknown
   Craftsman*; trans. Leach B.;
   Kodansha Int. Ltd. 1972.
9. Russell B., *Education & the Good
   Life* p. 165; Liveright Pub. Corp.
   (N.Y.) 1926.

CHAPTER TWELVE:
UNSELFISHNESS & COMPASSION
1. Cortazar J., *The Winners* p. 17;
   trans Kerrigan E.
2. Wolfe L. M., *John of the
   Mountains* p. 89; Univ. of
   Wisconsin Press 1979.
3. Schweitzer A., *My Life &
   Thought* p. 113; trans Campion C.
   T.; G. Allen & Unwin 1933.
4. Horney K., *The Neurotic
   Personality of our Time* p. 284;
   Routledge 1937.
5. Emerson R. W., *Essays* First
   Series, 1841.
6. Ullman J. R., *Man of Everest* p.
   307; G. Harrap 1955.
7. Smythe F. S., *The Spirit of the
   Hills* p. 173; Hodder & Stoughton
   1940.
8. Noyce C. W. F., *They Survived*;
   Heinemann 1962.
9. Hiebeler T., *North Face in Winter*;
   Barrie & Rockliff, 1962.
10. Koestler A., *Arrow in the Blue*.
11. An outstanding example of the

ideal expedition member was Dr.
Edward Wilson, one of Capt.
Scott's South Pole team. In many
ways he epitomizes the ideal
implicit in this book. For further
information see *South Pole
Odyssey*; ed. King H.; Blandford
Press 1982.
12. From a lecture by Dr. Payne J. to
   the Young Explorers' Trust
   Conference, Leeds 1978.
13. Quoted in Huxley E., *Scott of the
   Antarctic* p. 219; Pan Books 1979.
14. Worsley F. A., *Shackleton's Boat
   Journey*. p. 15; The Folio Society
   1974.
15. Chapman S., *Memoirs of a
   Mountaineer*; Chatto & Windus
   1945.
16. Prof. Fromm E., *Man for Himself*
   p. 107; Routledge & Kegan Paul.
17. Braddon R. *The Naked Island*;
   Pan 1952.
18. Schweitzer A., *My Life &
   Thought* p. 183; trans Campion C.
   T.: G. Allen & Unwin 1933.
19. Stevenson K. in correspondence
   with the author.

CHAPTER THIRTEEN:
HUMILITY & COURAGE
1. Hammarskjold D. *Markings* p.
   147; Faber & Faber 1964.
2. Ruskin J. *Modern Painters* v 3,
   4.16.24, 1860.
3. Wyatt J. *The Shining Levels* p. 82;
   Penguin Books 1973.
4. Huxley E. *Scott of the Antarctic* p.
   223; Pan Books 1979.
5. Bonatti W. *The Great Days* p. 137;
   Gollancz 1974.
6. Wainwright A. *A Pictorial Guide
   to the Lakeland Fells* Book 3: The
   Central Fells; postscript extract;
   The Westmorland Gazette 1958.
7. McTaggart D. *Greenpeace III* p.
   264; Collins 1978.
8. Moitoissier B. *The Long Way*;
   Adlard Coles 1974.
9. Forward by Garrett A. *Heavy
   Weather Sailing*; Adlard Coles
   1975.
10. *The Complete Works of Oscar*

Wilde intro.; Holland V.; Collins 1970.
11. Hemingway E.
12. Hammarskjold D. *Markings* p. 115; Faber & Faber 1964.
13. Lord Moran, *The Anatomy of Courage.*
14. Patton G. S. *War as I knew it* p. 340; HM (USA) 1947.
15. Kennedy J. F. *Profiles of Courage* p. 265-6 Harper & Row; Memorial Edition 1964.
16. Solzhenitsyn A. *Solzhenitsyn Speaks to the West*; Bodley Head 1978.
17. Prof. Meredith G. P., article *Personal Education*; Journal of Physical Education 1954.
18. Russell B. *Education & the Good Life* p. 69; H. Liveright 1954.
19. *Ibid* p. 62 & p. 66.
20. As 17 above.
21. The Daily Telegraph 25.2.81, p. 29.

CHAPTER FOURTEEN:
PHYSICAL DEVELOPMENT

1. *A Sound Mind in a Sound Body.* The concept of education through the physical.
2. *The case for Exercise* p. 4; Sports Council Research Working Papers No. 8.
3. *Ibid* p. 6.
4. 1977 Gallup Poll in USA showed almost 50% of adult population exercised daily; 55 million adults involved, and almost twice the percentage recorded in 1961.
5. *The Digest of Sports Statistics*; Sports Council; London 1983.
6. Newspaper report: The Sunday Times, 29.9.82.
7. *Ibid.*

CHAPTER FIFTEEN:
THE NATURAL ENVIRONMENT

1. Schumacher E. F. *Small is Beautiful* p. 118-9; Abacus Ed. Sphere Books 1973.
2. Chapman S. *Memoirs of a Mountaineer*; Chatto & Windus 1945.
3. Conrad J. *Lord Jim* p. 151-2; J. M. Dent & Sons 1948.
4. Teale E. W. *The Wilderness World of John Muir* p. 317; Houghton Mifflin (Boston USA) 1954.
5. The Daily Telegraph 14.8.82 p. 13.
6. As 4 above, p. 193.
7. Dr. Baker R. *The Mystery of Migration* p. 30; Harrow House 1980.
8. Report on BBC TV programme *Animal Olympians*; The Daily Telegraph 25.6.80.
9. The Daily Telegraph, 16.2.80.
10. The Daily Telegraph, 14.8.82.
11. Wolfe L. M. *'John of the Mountains'* p. 92; Univ. of Wisconsin Press 1979.
12. Prof. Watts A. *'Cloud Hidden Whereabouts Unknown'* p. 11; Abacus (Sphere Books Ltd) 1977.
13. Nansen F. *'Farthest North'* Vol. I. p. 390; A. Constable & Co. 1897.
14. As 11 above. p. 89.
15. Conway Sir M. *'The Alps'*; A. & C. Black, 1904.
16. Moittoissier B. *'The Long Way'* p. 78; Adlard Coles 1974.
17. *Ibid* p. 86.
18. Dr. Eiseley L. *The Immense Journey* pp. 16, 19; Vintage Books (Random House) (N.Y.) 1959.
19. Emerson R. W. *Education* 1882.
20. Thoreau H. D. *Walden*; Everyman's Library 1974.

CHAPTER SIXTEEN:
THE HOLISTIC APPROACH

1. The concise Oxford Dictionary p. 414; 7th ed. 1982. OUP.
2. Kaufman W. *The Portable Nietzsche*; Viking Press 1964.
3. Jacks L. P. *The Education of the Whole Man* p. 62; Univ. of London Press 1931.
4. Yanagi *The Unknown Craftsman* trans Leach B.; Kodansha Int. Ltd. 1972.
5. Rohe F. *The Zen of Running.* Random House (N.Y.) 1975.

6. Prof. Heath D. *Journal of Experiential Education* p. 8. vol. 1 1978 CU Box 249 Boulder, Colorado U.S.A. 80309.
7. Lee L. *Journal of Experiential Education* vol. I, 1978.
8. Prof. Watts A. *Cloud Hidden Whereabouts Unknown* p. 87; Abacus 1977.
9. Prof. Bronowski J. *The Identity of Man* p. 38; The Natural History Press N.Y. 1971.
10. Huxley A. *The Perennial Philosophy* p. 239-40; Fontana Books 1959.
11. Hammarskjold D. *Markings* p. 79; trans Auden W. H. & Sjoberg L.; Faber 1975.
12. *Ibid.*
13. Wordsworth W. *Tintern Abbey* lines 93-102.
14. Wyatt J. *The Shining Levels* p. 132; Penguin 1976.
15. Smythe F. S. *The Spirit of the Hills*; Hodder & Stoughton 1940.
16. Moittoissier B. *The Long Way* p. 124; Adlard Coles 1974.
17. Rousseau J. J. *Emile* book 2.

CHAPTER SEVENTEEN:
A CONCEPT OF MATURITY

1. The Concise Oxford Dictionary p. 626; 7th ed. 1982 (OUP).
2. Maslow A. H. *Motivation & Personality*; Harper and Row 1970.
3. Young P. T. *Motivation & Emotion* p. 454-456; Wiley 1961 (Quoted in Arnold P. J. *Education, P.E. & Personality*; Heinemann 1972.)
4. Rörs H. *Kurt Hahn* p. xiii; Routledge & Kegan Paul 1970.
5. Huxley A. *The Perennial Philosophy* p. 126; Fontana Books 1959.
6. Prof. Meredith G. P., article *Personal Education*, Journal of Physical Education 1954.
7. Emerson R. W. *Self-Reliance* Essays: First Series.
8. Prof. Heath D., *Journal of Experiential Education* vol. I, 1978.
9. Hodgkin R. A. *Born Curious* p. 3; John Wiley 1976.
10. Sir Hunt J. *Life is Meeting* Hodder & Stoughton 1978.
11. See 6. above.
12. Frontispiece, College of Buddhist Studies literature; Ulverston; Cumbria.
13. Vincent L. article *PE's contribution to the Mental Health of Students* Journal of Health and PE; April 1933.
14. Meister Eckart (1300 a.d.).
15. Leonard G., *The Ultimate Athlete* p. 97; Viking Press (N.Y.) 1975.

CHAPTER EIGHTEEN:
IN PURSUIT OF HAPPINESS

1. Emerson R. W. *Essays: First Series.*
2. Buddha – quoted in foreword *Man for Himself*; Prof. Fromm E. Routledge & Kegan Paul 1949.
3. Johnson P., *Enemies of Society*; Weidenfeld & Nicolson 1977.
4. Smythe F. S. *The Spirit of the Hills* p. 170; Hodder & Stoughton 1940.
5. Newspaper Report on Essex University 1972.
6. Service R. *More Selected Verse* p. 1; Dodd Mead & Co., (N.Y.) 1960.
7. Tasker J. *Savage Arena* p. 125; Methuen, London 1982.
8. Aeschylus *Agamemnon* 458 BC.
9. Roy Memorial address, Delhi; quoted in *Resurgence* No. 83, Nov. 1980.
10. Lecture to students by Buddhist monk 1979.
11. The Bhagavad Gita; 4; Penguin Books 1962.
12. Newspaper interview; The Sunday Times 6.1.80.
13. Roos W. D. *North West Passage* p. 196-197; Hollis & Carter 1980.
14. Prof. Fromm E. *Man for Himself* p. 181; Routledge & Kegan Paul 1948.
15. *Ibid* p. 189.
16. Scott D. article *On the Profundity Trail*, Mountain 15.

17. Prof. Watts A. *Cloud Hidden Whereabouts Unknown* p. 30; Abacus 1977.
18. Information from the Wrekin Trust, Dove House, Little Birch, Herefordshire.
19. Patterson C. H. *Foundations for a theory of Instruction* p. 8; Harper & Rowe USA 1977.
20. Wyatt J. *The Shining Levels* p. 45; Penguin Books 1973.
21. From comments to author by Lloynes C., editor, Journal of Adventure Ed.
22. Schweitzer A. *My Life & Thought* p. 268; trans Campion C. T.; Allen & Unwin 1933.
23. Kierkegaard S. *Fear and Trembling and the Sickness unto Death* Princeton University Press 1974.
24. Back R. *Jonathan Livingstone Seagull* p. 83; Pan Books 1975.
25. Quotations, Argus Posters.

275; 1897.
11. See 9. above p. 53.
12. Young G. W.; *The Influence of Mountains on the Development of Human Intelligence*; pamphlet; Jackson; Glasgow 1957.
13. Smythe F. S. *The Spirit of the Hills* p. 37; Hodder & Stoughton 1940.
14. Stack P. *Island Quest – The Inner Hebrides* p. 27; Collins 1979.
15. Lowe B. *The Beauty of Sport* p. 192; Prentice Hall 1977.
16. Smythe F. S. *The Spirit of the Hills* p. 170; Hodder & Stoughton 1940.
17. Hammarskjold D. *Markings* p. 84; trans Auden W. H. & Sjoberg L.; Faber 1975.
18. Prof. Whitehead A. N. *Adventures of Ideas* p. 360; Cambridge Univ. Press 1939.

CHAPTER NINETEEN:
THE UNIVERSAL QUEST

1. Philo, quoted in Huxley A. *The Perennial Philosophy* pp. 305-6; Fontana 1959.
2. Teale E. W. *The Wilderness World of John Muir* pp. 318-319; Houghton Mifflin (Boston USA) 1964.
3. Visvinatha quoted in Huxley A. *The Perennial Philosophy* p. 147; Fontana 1959.
4. Barbellion W. N. P. *Enjoying Life & Other Literary Remains* 1919.
5. Wyatt J. *The Shining Levels* p. 22; Penguin Books 1973.
6. Moittoissier B. *The Long Way* p. 126; Adlard Coles 1974.
7. Van Der Post L. *Yet Being Someone Other* p. 180; Hogarth Press 1982.
8. Marshall R. *Alaskan Wilderness* p. 38; Univ. of California Press 1970.
9. Wolfe L. M. *John of the Mountains* pp. 38-39; Univ. of Wisconsin Press 1979.
10. Nansen F. *Farthest North* vol. 1 p.

Index

148

Notes

PRINTED BY MARTINS THE PRINTERS LTD, BERWICK UPON TWEED